I'm in the Wine Store Now What?!™

by Peter Morrell

SILVER LINING BOOKS

NEW YORK

introduction

There you are in the wine shop with hundreds—maybe thousands—of bottles of wine to choose from. As a retail wine merchant for the past 35 years, I know your concerns, and very possibly, your confusion. All those unusual names, the vast array of labels, all the different years and strange terms like "cru." Where to begin?

My advice? Relax, help is at hand—and I guarantee you'll find learning about wine as enjoyable as drinking it—well, almost! My goal in writing this book is to supply information that will help you maximize your pleasure when purchasing and drinking wine—without jargon, without esoteric concepts and most of all, without snobbery.

In fact, I can't emphasize enough how much I dislike wine snobbery. Plenty of good wine is available between $7 and $15—and always will be. Many American jug wines are as refreshing and flavorful as a French wine with a fancy name. For under $15, you can find any number of great tasting wines from all over the world, and learning about these can be a happy, fascinating experience.

Throughout the book, I suggest wines for every variety and region, which we've called "Peter Selects". For the most part, I've kept my picks under $20. They include many of my favorites, but with the knowledge you're about to gain, you'll soon be able to experiment successfully on your own.

So read on—and let the book take you on a journey into the wonderfully rich and satisfying world of wine.

Peter Morrell
Morrell and Company

table of contents

Wine Basics

what is wine?

*Grape juice
or nectar from
the gods?*

Great, you are ready to learn about wine! That says a lot about you—no doubt you've enjoyed wine with meals, and probably bought a few bottles. But chances are that like most people, you often feel overwhelmed by the subject of wine . . . all the different regions, names, vintages. It's hard to keep it all straight. What's a person to do? Relax. The good news is that learning about wine is fun as well as fascinating. So start tasting and get ready to explore the wonderful world of wine.

Exactly what is wine, you ask? Wine is fermented grape juice. The operative word is fermented, which refers to the process of **fermentation**, or the conversion of all that sugary grape juice into alcohol, thanks to a bit of yeast. Where does the yeast come from?

It's a natural fungus that grows on grape skins. In the late 1800s, winemakers started adding sugar-eating yeast to the process, to better control fermentation.

For the most part, wine is fermented in wooden oak barrels or steel vats. Next comes the big decision: how long to **age** it and at what temperature. And that's up to the **vintner,** or winemaker. Depending on the grape, the vintage, and the style of vinification, some wine can be drunk almost immediately, while others require years of aging.

There are about 25 **varietals,** or varieties of grapes, used by winemakers around the world. Each variety has a name. Now here's where it gets tricky. Sometimes a wine is named after the grape's variety—for example, Cabernet Sauvignon; sometimes it is named for the region where the grape was grown, such as Bordeaux. Yes, this can cause some confusion, but you'll get the hang of it.

More basic facts: wine comes in two primary colors, red and white. (Pink or rosé wine is considered a secondary hue, not a color in itself.) Wine comes in different styles: **still** (meaning no bubbles, what most of us think of when we think of wine), **sparkling** (wine with bubbles, such as Champagne), **dessert** (sweet-tasting wine), and **fortified** (wine with extra alcohol added).

GETTING STARTED TASTING WINE

As with any other taste you've developed, you need to build familiarity with wine. Begin by purchasing a mixed case—or 12 bottles—of different varietals, or types of wine. Have your local wine store merchant put one together for you. Tell him or her you don't want to spend more than $130 for the case. You want six reds and six whites. (You may get a 10% discount for buying a case.) A mixed case will allow you to experience a myriad of flavors from the differing varietal wines. This is a good way to find out quickly if you prefer one varietal over another.

white wine
at a glance

*From white to
pale green
and shades in
between*

White wine is best defined by what it lacks. In other words, white wine is wine without the red pigment that makes red wine red. (The red pigment comes from red grape skins. More on that on pages 42–43.) White wine is rarely, if ever, purely white or clear. In fact, the color of white wine can range from light yellow to gold, and is sometimes even pale green. Popular white wine varieties include Chardonnay, Sauvignon Blanc, Riesling, and Pinot Grigio. You'll learn much more about white wine in chapter 2.

White wine is often (but not always) made from the juice of white grapes, which are not really white but can be greenish, greenish yellow, golden yellow, or even pinkish yellow. It can also, occasionally, be made with the juice of red grapes, but only the juice of the grapes, not the skins. The juice of most red or purple grapes has no red pigmentation, so a wine made with only the juice of a red grape can be a white wine.

When compared to red wine, white wine is often described as less **full-bodied** (body is the word winetasters refer to when describing a wine's flavor, richness, and depth). At the same time, whites have their own "personalities." They can range from **soft** (meaning a smooth taste) to **crisp** (a little tart), to **broad** (flavor intensive). Yes, wine has a unique terminology. See Talking About Wine on page 68 for definitions.

ASK THE EXPERTS

Why is white wine chilled before it is served, and how cold should it be?
White wine should be served slightly chilled, but not so cold that its flavor is dulled. Aim for about 45 degrees F (about the average in most refrigerators), certainly noticeably cooler than room temperature.

Why is white wine so popular as a cocktail?
In America, dry white wine has become a popular **aperitif**, or predinner drink. This popularity blossomed in the 1970s, when a number of excellent California white wines started coming on the market. Diners felt that the lightness of a white wine was an ideal way to prepare the **palate** (the way your mouth senses taste) for the various flavors of the meal to come.

red wine
at a glance

*Just add
skins to create
complexity*

The first obvious difference between white wine and red wine is color. Just as white wine isn't really white, red wine isn't necessarily red. It ranges in color from dark pink to ruby to purple to almost black, with a bit of orange and blue thrown in. To produce red wine, winemakers leave in the skins of the red grapes while fermenting the juice. The skins contain **tannin**, a natural substance that makes red wine taste "firm" and creates that puckering sensation in the back of the mouth after the first swallow.

The second difference is that red wines are usually more **complex** than white. What is complex? It means that when you drink it, you taste more flavors and sensations in your mouth. More important, complexity is something that the vintners create. Complexity depends on a number of things: the grape varieties used, as well as the **vintage** (the year the grapes were harvested and turned into wine), the health of the grapes, the winemaking method, the wine's acid level, and the amount of time the wine spent aging in the barrel or steel vat.

ASK THE EXPERTS

Why do red wines taste so astringent, compared to white wines?
That's because red wine has more tannin than white wine. Tannin comes primarily from grapes' skins, seeds, and stems. White wine is fermented without the skins, so it has much less tannin than red wines. To balance the tannin taste, have some soft creamy cheese with your red wine and see how well they pair up together.

Does it take longer to make reds than whites?
It takes about the same amount of time to make a red as a white. However, winemakers usually age reds in barrels longer than whites.

Why do people tend to serve red wine with meat?
There are no hard and fast rules about serving red wines with meat, but the usually acknowleged rule of thumb is: like with like. Because red wines taste complex or full-flavored, they stand up well to food that is equally full-bodied, such as steak, lamb chops, or roast fowl.

pink wine
at a glance

*Don't blush
over a rosé*

In addition to red and white wines, there is pink wine—formally known as **rosé** wine and nowadays often referred to as **blush** wine. Pink wines are usually made from red grapes. To make the wine pink, the winemaker leaves the grape juice in contact with the red skins for only a very short time, a few hours or days as compared to several weeks for a deep red wine.

In some cases, pink wine is made by combining red and white grapes, or by blending red and white wine at various stages of the winemaking process. Some French winemakers, for example, make superb rosé Champagne by combining red and white grapes. One of the more famous pink wines is called, confusingly, White Zinfandel. Despite its name, White Zinfandel is a rosé wine made with the juice from red Zinfandel grapes. Even though White Zinfandel wine has had only minimal contact with its grapes' red skins, it's enough to turn its color from white to pink. Why they are called white zinfandels instead of rosé or pink remains a mystery.

A popular old favorite pink wine is Mateus, a medium-dry rosé wine from Portugal (see page 152). It was the rage in the '70s, when European wines were beginning to gain popularity in the United States.

In general, pink wines tend to be light-bodied and somewhat sweet. Many experts often dismiss rosé wines, claiming they lack the complexity of red wine and the "personality" of good white wine. This is unfortunate, because rosé wines can be quite delicious, and appropriate—even perfect—for many occasions, such as showers, brunch parties, and outdoor summer celebrations.

FIRST PERSON DISASTER

In the Pink

When I hosted a baby shower luncheon for my cousin (who had announced that she was expecting a baby girl), a guest brought me a bottle of pink wine as a hostess gift. I laughed when she gave it to me, thinking that pink wine was sort of "camp"—right up there with pink champagne. She appeared offended at my laughter. Because of the hurt expression on her face, I later checked at my local wine shop. I learned that she had brought me a very expensive bottle of rosé wine. I tried it a week later and it was delicious. I was so embarrassed that I wrote her an effusive thank you note to cover for my rude behavior. Now whenever I'm invited to a festive occasion or a brunch I always bring a bottle of pink wine.

—Trish L., Hoboken, New Jersey

sparkling wine
at a glance

The art and science of putting bubbles in wine

A sparkling wine is still wine infused with bubbles from carbon dioxide gas. The fast way to do this calls for winemakers to simply inject carbon dioxide into a bottle of wine, much as soda makers do when they make soda. At one time, American winemakers did just that and created sweet inexpensive wines, such as cold duck, that were big on fizziness and low on taste.

To create a sparkling wine that is fizzy but not too fizzy, and very high on taste, requires a much more refined technique developed by the French called *méthode champenoise*. This traditional way of making champagne requires the wine to be **fermented** twice. The first fermentation (where yeast is added to turn the sugar into alcohol and carbon dioxide, the latter of which escapes into the air) takes place in an oak barrel. The second fermentation takes place in the bottle, where a bit of sugar and wine (the French call it a **liqueur de tirage**) are added and the subsequent bubbles (from the carbon dioxide) are trapped in the bottle. The result is a sparkling wine rich in taste, with bubbles that infuse its very being. Only if it is made in the French region of Champagne (see page 104), does it get to be called Champagne with a capital C.

In between the fast and slow ways of making sparkling wine lies the vat, or **charmat**, process. Here vats of wine are put into pressurized tanks so the carbon dioxide created during fermentation is retained. Vat fermentation produces some sparkling wines that can cost from $5.00 to $10.00.

ASK THE EXPERTS

I've only had Champagne at weddings when they cut the cake. What else can you serve with it?

Many people pair Champagne with wedding cake, and while that is not an ideal match because the Champagne is dry and the cake is sweet, it's still a lovely tradition. While Champagne is a "high acid" wine and would fight with very rich foods, it does go well with dishes like grilled sole, chicken, and veal piccata.

How many people does a bottle of Champagne serve?

Champagne is often just served for toasting. The rule of thumb is six glasses per one bottle. A party of 100 people would require 17 bottles for one toast. Add extra to be safe.

dessert wine
at a glance

How sweet it is

Dessert wines are rich, intensely sweet wines. Virtually all dessert wines are developed from grapes harvested late in the season and are therefore that much sweeter. Moreover, the flavors of many dessert wines are further enhanced by the help of a fungus called *Botrytis cinerea,* known in the wine world as **noble rot**. It attacks ripe grapes late in the autumn and causes the grapes' water to evaporate, leaving a very sweet flavor. The flavors can range from honeylike to caramel, apricot, or peach.

Almost every wine-growing region of the world has a sweet dessert wine, some more famous than others. Dessert wines include Ausleses from Germany, Sauternes from France, Vins Santo from Italy, Tokay wines from Hungary, Moscatel from Portugal, and late-harvest wines from the United States.

DESSERT WINE PRIMER

Here are a few of the better-known sweet wines

Sauternes: the best-known dessert wines. They serve as a benchmark for quality among sweet wines, with Chateau d'Yquem reigning as the queen. Coming from the Bordeaux (see page 92) region of France, Sauternes are rich and fruit-filled, with an apricot, pineapple, or peach flavor overlaid with a creamy quality.

Eiswein (Ice wine): a German dessert wine is created when grapes are allowed to remain on the vine until winter temperatures freeze them. They are then pressed, and the frozen water is left behind, creating a concentrated syrup with pure fruit flavors and sharp acidity.

Beerenauslese and Trockenbeerenauslese wines: considered Germany's greatest wines. Unlike eiswein, these are produced through the effects of botrytis. They are luscious, low alcohol wines, with vivid fruit flavors.

Because of the infrequent perfect weather conditions necessary to produce Beerenauslese and Trockenbeerenauslese, these very special sweet wines are invariably expensive.

Tokay: a sweet white wine from the Tokaj region of Hungary that rivals the best sweet wines of France and other regions. They are created with botrytis-affected grapes.

Late Harvest: the term American winemakers use for their sweet wines. Many are enhanced by botrytis.

Vin Santo: a sweet wine from Tuscany made from bunches of grapes that are harvested, then allowed to hang from hooks in the hot attics of the winery (or on straw mats) until they shrivel and are then pressed. The result is a unique sweet wine with almondlike flavor.

 SK THE EXPERTS

Do dessert wines go with desserts?
Yes. You want to match flavor for flavor. A sweet dessert wine is ideal with a rich, sweet dessert, but also try serving them with fresh fruits such as peaches, cantaloupe, or berries

Should I chill a dessert wine before serving?
Ideally, no. Chilling wine inhibits its flavors. It is recommended for white wine because chilling softens its acidity. Dessert wines are often low in acidity and may be served at room temperature.

fortified wine
at a glance

When alcohol is added to wine

Fortified wines derive their name from the fact that they are **fortified**, or strengthened, with alcohol—usually brandy. Fortified wines include Sherry, Port, Madeira, and Marsala. These fortifed wines can be either sweet or dry (which is wine-speak for the opposite of sweet). Dry varieties are best enjoyed as **aperitifs** (a beverage served before dinner to stimulate the appetite), and sweet fortified wines double as dessert wines.

Fortified wines, especially Madeira and Sherry, are also frequently used in cooking, adding fabulous, distinctive flavors to soups and sauces. Certain dishes, such as chicken marsala, even feature fortified wine. But beware—fortified wines have very strong flavors, so they should be used sparingly. If the correct amount is not specified in the recipe, start by adding a tablespoon of wine at a time to the dish, then adjust to taste.

While many fortified wines originated in particular regions of the world (Sherry from Spain, for example, and Port from Portugal), today these wines are also produced in Australia, South Africa, the United States, and other New World wine-growing regions. Experts agree, however, that the best fortified wines are usually those that come from their original regions.

FORTIFIED WINE PRIMER
Some of the best-known fortified wines include:

Madeira: named for the Portuguese-owned island where it is made. Subjected to a lengthy heating process during maturation, it ranges in color from pale gold to gold and can be dry (called Malmsey) or very sweet (called Rainwater).

Marsala: Italy's most famous fortified wine. Marsala, made in Sicily, has a rich flavor that can be either sweet or dry. Dry Marsala is used in chicken and veal dishes. Sweet Marsala is used for desserts, such as Italian zabaglione.

Port: originally developed in northern Portugal. There are many types of Port, but it is basically a sweet wine fortified with grape alcohol (brandy). It creates a robust, sweet wine that is the perfect afterdinner drink.

Sherry: originally made in the Andalusia region of southern Spain. Sherries range in color, flavor, and sweetness from bone dry (for before meals) and light to rich and creamy (after dinner).

Vin Doux Naturel: from southern France. These wines are high in natural sugar and then fortified with extra alcohol. They are always sweet and are enjoyed as a dessert wine.

answers to common questions

Can the quality of wine be determined by price?
The short answer is no. An inexpensive wine can taste just as lovely as an expensive one. Price is due to a number of factors: the quantity of that particular wine (some years there are low-yield harvests and so less wine is made), the quality of the wine-making, and public perception. Price is also a by-product of marketing. Most of us think a great-tasting wine has to be expensive and some marketers take advantage of that.

Does drinking red wine cause headaches more frequently than drinking white wine?
Research indicates that red wine is a common trigger for those prone to migraine headaches. The real culprit is the tannins (acids that are natural to red grape skins and stems, and to the oak barrels that wines age in). If you think the tannins are the reason for your red-wine headaches, then stick to white wines, which are low in tannins. Or try those reds that are low in tannin, such as lighter Pinot Noirs (see page 46) and Beaujolais (see page 49).

Why does it say on the back of most wine labels "contains sulfites"?
To control the growth of natural bacteria in the wild yeasts that grow naturally on grape skins, and to preserve a wine's shelf life, winemakers add a bit of sulfur dioxide during the winemaking process and when a wine is bottled. U.S. law requires that winemakers list any additives. Some people are sensitive to sulfites, due to allergies. However, sulfur dioxide is virtually indispensible in the winemaking process.

I have a bit of red wine left over from a month ago. I took a sip and it tasted terrible. Can I could use it for cooking?
Bad wine is bad wine, whether it is sipped from a glass or is part of a sauce. In fact, a bad wine will ruin your dish! With the exception of fortified wines, which tend to keep well once opened, always use as freshly opened a wine for cooking as you would for drinking.

White wines need to be chilled, but what about reds?

Red wine should *not* be drunk cold because cooling makes the tannin in it taste bitter. On the other hand, it should not be served too warm. Ideally, the wine should be about 65 degrees F, and the bottle should feel slightly cool to the touch.

How many calories are in a glass of wine?

Get ready for some bad news. There are about 120 calories in a four-ounce glass of wine, be it red or white. For a six-ounce glass of wine, we're really talking 180 calories. Eight ounces of plain old grape juice or soda is only 100 calories. The good news is that wine is definitely less fattening than spirits, such as gin or rum. Four ounces of gin is 280 calories.

HELFPUL RESOURCES

BOOKS

Beginner's Guide to Understanding Wine
By Michael Schuster
Simon & Schuster

The Complete Idiot's Guide to Wine
By Philip Seldon
Macmillan Publishing Company

Wine for Dummies
By Ed McCarthy and Mary Ewing-Mulligan
IDG

Wine Lover's Companion
By Ron Herbst and Sharon Tyler Herbst
Barron's

2

White Grape
varieties

muscat

gewürztraminer

chardonnay

pinot grigio

about white
grape varieties

*The top white
grape varietals*

Hundreds of white grape varieties are used to make white wine
the world over, but only a few varietals are so delicious that they
are known by their grape name. The all-star white wine **varietals,**
or types, are: Chardonnay, Sauvignon Blanc, Chenin Blanc, and
Riesling.

Of the many factors that go into making a wine, it is the grape variety that determines its fundamental characteristics. For something
so important, it can be puzzling why winemakers are less than clear
about them. One reason is that in some countries a wine is named
after the region it originates from, while in other countries it is

named for the grape varietal. For example, a Californian wine made from Chardonnay grapes will be called a Chardonnay, while in France, some Chardonnay wines will be called after the region where the grapes are grown—for example, Chablis or Meursault. So what makes a bottle of Meursault different from a bottle of Chablis? Good question. The answer lies in the soil and microclimates of each region, as well as the technique and skill of the grower and winemaker: how he plants and when he harvests the grapes, how and where he ferments or ages the wine, in old or new oak or perhaps in steel vats, then how long he ages the bottle before he sells it. It's much more art than science.

 **SK THE EXPERTS**

Is acidity important in a white wine?
Although all wines, be they red, white, or pink, contain acid, it is most important in white wines. White wines with a significant level of acid will taste **crisp**, while those with low acid taste **soft**. This is not to imply that crispness is good and softness bad. A white wine with too much acid can taste coarse instead of crisp. It all comes down to personal preferences. Some people like crisp, some don't.

Does white wine only taste good with white meats?
White wine works well with lighter foods, typically white meat, fish, and cream-based pastas. Why? Because the lighter body of white wine matches better with lighter fare than a red wine, which is typically more full-bodied. Again, it's a matter of personal taste. An oft-followed guideline is to match the color of the sauce to the wine: red sauces with red wine, white sauces with white.

chardonnay

The leading white wine grape

Almost anyone who has ever drunk a glass of wine, if asked to name a white wine, would say Chardonnay. It is grown throughout the world, most famously in France, where for centuries it has been grown as the white wine grape of Burgundy (including the Chablis district). Today, Chardonnay grapes are also cultivated in several other European regions, including Italy, Spain, and Bulgaria, as well as extensively in the United States, Australia, South America, and, to a lesser degree, New Zealand.

Why is Chardonnay so popular with winemakers? Perhaps it's because the grape has a subtle **personality**, which allows subsoil minerals and nutrients to influence its flavor and permits wine-makers to build complexity into it, using a number of common winemaking techniques. The most common involve fermenting the wine in oak barrels. The newer the barrel, the oakier the wine will taste; the older the barrel, the more subtle the oak influence. Other winemakers elect to ferment it in steel barrels, which makes the Chardonnay taste flintier and crisper than oak-aged wines.

Flavors of Chardonnay

At its best, Chardonnay features bold, rich, fruit flavors like apple, fig, melon, pear, peach, pineapple, and citrus. It also may possess hints of spice, honey, butter, vanilla, butterscotch, and hazelnut. Most signifi-cantly, as a result of oak-barrel aging, Chardonnay is well known for its oak-accented flavors, which are usually described as vanilla and toast.

ASK THE EXPERTS

Is a Chardonnay always a Chardonnay?

Much to the surprise of many consumers, many wines that go by another name are actually made from Chardonnay grapes. These include: Chablis from the French village of Chablis, White Burgundy wines from the Côte de Beaune—such as the exquisite whites of Chassagne and Puligny—Montrachet and Meursault, plus Rully, Mercurey, Pouilly-Fuissé, and Mâcon, all from the more southern parts of Burgundy.

Where does a Chardonnay's oaky flavor come from?

That unique taste comes from the oak barrels in which it's often fermented and aged. No other white wine benefits as much from oak aging or barrel fermentation as Chardonnay. The best Chardonnays are fermented and aged in barrels made of new or partially new French oak. Some vintners prefer to ferment in older casks that have lost most of their oaky character but still convey a subtle oak essence. Today some large wineries, especial-ly those in Australia, put oak chips to soak in their lower-priced Chardonnays—a quick way to give a wine a bit of oaky flavor.

sauvignon blanc

A strong favorite

In France, the Sauvignon Blanc grape is grown in two important wine regions: Bordeaux and the Loire Valley. In Bordeaux, the best dry whites come from a district with gravelly subsoil, called Graves. In other parts of Bordeaux, the Sauvignon Blanc-based dry whites are marketed simply as Bordeaux Blanc. In the Loire, the best Sauvignon Blanc wines originate in the wine districts of Sancerre or Pouilly-Fumé. Sauvignon Blanc is also grown in Italy, the United States, New Zealand, South America, and South Africa.

When mediocre, Sauvignon Blanc can come across as simply a generic white wine. When it is well made, however, it is a strong, dry, white wine with lovely citrus, often grassy, overtones. It serves as a nice alternative to Chardonnay, especially since it is often less expensive. Why? Mostly because wine marketers are trying to make it more competitive with the ever-popular Chardonnay. Again, price often has little to do with the taste of a wine.

The Flavor of Sauvignon Blanc

Sauvignon Blanc at its best is brisk and light-bodied, and features citrus and floral scents. Most Sauvignon Blanc wines are dry and **unoaked** (fermented in steel vats instead of oak barrels), with a bracing, lively acidity that balances the wine's natural fruitiness.

ASK THE EXPERTS

What is the difference between Sauvignon Blanc and Chardonnay?

Sauvignon Blanc grapes are often higher in acidity than Chardonnay grapes, giving the wine a crisper, lighter quality. In California, some of the best wines are aged in oak, so they will have a slightly oaky overtone. In France, however, most Sauvignon Blancs are not oak-aged, making them taste even crisper. To many wine lovers, Chardonnay and Sauvignon Blanc are equally delicious wines. See for yourself: buy a bottle of each and compare the differences.

How long will a bottle of Sauvignon Blanc keep?

Some very fine white Burgundys, such as Montrachet and the best Meursaults, are made to be bought young and stored, sometimes for years. In fact, the longer they are stored, the richer they taste. Not so with Sauvignon Blanc wines. Drink them soon after you buy them.

chenin blanc

A bipolar reputation

Another native of France's Loire Valley, Chenin Blanc has a sort of schizophrenic reputation. At home in France, it serves as the basis for two very famous white wines, Vouvray and Anjou. However, when cultivated outside of France (especially in the United States and in South Africa), it loses some of its specialness, becoming merely a rather everyday blending grape.

Some experts believe that it will eventually find its niche in certain parts of California and, as a result, grow more popular. In South Africa (where it is known as Steen) it is already considered one of the region's more important grapes, and is used not only in table wine but also in fortified wines (that is, Ports and Sherries).

The Flavor of Chenin Blanc

Chenin Blanc's signature is its acidity, combined with high alcohol and a full-bodied, almost oily texture. Though Chenin Blanc is most often found in simple, dry wines, it can—especially in the Loire Valley—create great wines in a variety of styles from dry to sweet. It has a subtle fruitiness (melon, peach, quince, apricot, and sometimes even a citrus quality.) It can have spicy overtones together with a smooth hint of honey. Well-made Chenin Blanc wines age well.

PETER SELECTS

- **Vouvray Château de Monfort**
  (Loire Valley, France)
  $8 - $10

- **Vouvray Cuvée de Silex Domaine des Aubuissières**
  (Loire Valley, France)
  $15 - $17

VOUVRAY

Chenin Blanc produces a very special wine, called Vouvray (pronounced voo-vray), for the village of the same name in the Loire Valley. The wines of Vouvray come in several styles: dry, medium-dry, or sweet (called moelleux). There is also a sparkling Vouvray. The best sweet Vouvray wines need years to develop and can last a long time because of their remarkable acidity.

riesling

Germany's finest

After Chardonnay, perhaps the greatest white wine grape is the Riesling. It is best known for producing wines in many regions of Germany, with the wines from the Rheingau and Mosel regions considered the purest expression. Riesling grapes are also cultivated in Alsace (France), Austria, California, Oregon, Washington, New York's Finger Lakes region, Canada, Australia, New Zealand, South Africa, and South America. You can spot all Rieslings in winestores fairly easily thanks to the distinctive shape of their tall, slender bottles, which are either brown or green.

True noble Rieslings have delicacy, complexity, and longevity. Riesling's reputation has suffered, however, in part because certain wines marketed as Riesling—including Grey Riesling and Sylvaner Riesling—are made with inferior grapes.

The Flavors of Riesling

Commonly, Riesling produces light-bodied, dry (or medium-dry), low-alcohol wines, often with bracing acidity and crispness. A good Riesling has a distinctive floral or honeysuckle aroma with citrus (lime), peach, and apple. For the most part, Rieslings should not be aged. They should be consumed fresh and young.

PETER SELECTS

- **Hugel Riesling**
  (Alsace, France) $15 - $17

- **Bernkasteler Kurfurstlay Riesling**
  (Mosel, Germany) $8-$15

- **Rudesheimer Berg Riesling**
  (Rheingau, Germany) $25

- **Argyle Dry Riesling**
  (Oregon, USA) $12 - $14

FOOD & WINE

Riesling is a marvelous "food wine;" whether dry or off-dry, it goes with just about any meal, from roast pork to shellfish. For example, Alsatian Riesling is the classic wine with choucroute garni (an Alsatian and German specialty featuring pork sausages and sauerkraut). Similarly, lighter Rieslings pair well with virtually all Asian cuisines such as Chinese, Thai, Vietnamese, or Burmese, and go particularly well with Indian food, whether sweet or hot.

gewürztraminer

A grape with character

Gewürztraminer (pronounced ga-VERZ-tra-mee-ner) is German for "spicy grape from Tramin." (Tramin is a little village in Northern Italy where the grape originated.) Nowadays, Gewürztraminer grapes are grown throughout the world, most famously in the Alsace region of France, as well as in California and Italy. Only a small amount is grown and made into wine in Germany.

In any case, the variety, which can be temperamental to grow, needs a relatively cool climate in order to ripen properly. The appreciation of Gewürztraminer wine is said to be an "acquired taste" that calls for a special fondness for its spicy nature and, often, mineral and earthy flavors.

Flavors of Gewürztraminer

Full-bodied and flamboyant, Gewürztraminer wines are invariably deeply flavored, aromatic wines. Their flavor is somewhat exotic with a bit of fruitiness (apricot), floral (rose), and herbal spice. Still, they are dry, refreshing wines that couple extremely well with food. Left for late harvest, Gewürztraminer (especially in Alsace) makes a rich, exotic, complex dessert wine (see pages 18–19 for additional dessert wine recommendations). Gewürztraminers are easy to spot in a wine store by the shape of their bottles. Look for tall, slender brown or green bottles.

FIRST PERSON DISASTER

Good memories gone sour

When I was a young student, I traveled to Germany for a year on a scholarship and discovered their wonderful wines. One of my favorites was a wine called Liebfraumilch, which I learned means "milk of the virgin." It was a light white wine, which went well with the inexpensive meals I was eating. Over there it was very cheap and plentiful. That wine became a symbol of my year in Germany and so before I left for the States, I bought a bottle to take home. I planned on saving it for a special occasion. The event came: graduation, three years later. Unfortunately, when I opened the bottle and tasted it, the wine was not nearly as good as I remembered. In fact it was downright sour. I asked a friend of mine who is a wine buff and he said Liebfraumilch should never be stored for very long. It should be drunk as soon as possible. Only memories improve with age, not light white wines.

—Alan C., Cincinnatti, Ohio

other white varietals

A world of white

As you experiment with white wine, don't limit yourself to the better known whites. Try these varieties to get a full appreciation of what white has to offer.

Pinot Grigio/Pinot Gris

Pinot Grigio or Pinot Gris (different names for the same grape) makes wines with a slighty deeper color than most whites. (An exception is the Italian Pinot Grigio wines, which are often quite pale.) It is cultivated in France, where it is called Pinot Gris; in Germany, Rulander; in France's Alsace, Tokay Pinot Gris. Pinot Gris wines tend to be medium-to-full-bodied wines, lightly fruity, somewhat peachy, with perhaps a hint of spice.

Sémillon

Sémillon is a white grape with its origins in Bordeaux. Often it is blended with Sauvignon Blanc, and forms the basis of whites found in France's Graves and Pessac-Léognan regions, as well as Australia's Hunter Valley. Sémillon boasts a rich, honeyed flavor with complex fig and pear notes. In the Sauternes region of

Bordeaux, Sémillon is vinted sweet as a late-harvest or dessert wine.

Pinot Blanc

Considered a poor man's Chardonnay, Pinot Blanc nonetheless makes a fine white wine, just not as complex. It is grown in Champagne, Burgundy, Alsace, Germany, Italy, and California. When well made, it is intense, concentrated, and complex, with ripe pear, spice, citrus, and honey notes. It can age, but it is best drunk early while its fruit is still vibrant.

Melon de Bourgogne

After Chardonnay and Sauvignon Blanc, it is among France's most planted white grape varieties, almost totally because of the popularity of the delicately dry, light Muscadet wine, from a region at the mouth of the Loire River in France. The region produces a light, delicate, fresh wine that is a delightful accompaniment to seafood, especially shellfish.

 **ASK THE EXPERTS**

What makes a white wine good?

A good wine, be it white or red, has what wine makers call **balance**. This means that the acidity and tannin (there is a bit in white wine), which give white wine its backbone are balanced with the softer amounts of sugar and alcohol in the wine.

How can you tell if a white wine is bad?

These are a number of things to look for. First, use your nose and sniff. Bad wines give off a chemical, bacterial, or moldy odor. Taster beware. If the wine smells flat or cooked, it's been **oxidized**, meaning too much air got into the bottle and ruined the wine. Take a sip. If it's vinegar-tasting, then the wine has "turned"—literally, into vinegar. Finally, note the cork. If it's moldy or smells off, like damp cardboard, it's a bad cork which usually, but not always, means a bad (corked) wine.

answers to common questions

Sometimes I don't have time to chill a bottle of white wine. Can you put ice cubes in a glass of white wine?

Yes, but then fish them out after a few minutes. Otherwise, when the ice melts it will dilute the wine's flavor. If you need to chill a bottle quickly, put it in the freezer for no more than 15 minutes. (Just don't forget it!)

I was planning on having a party and chilled all this white wine, but had to call off the party. Can I take the wine out of the refrigerator and put it back in my wine rack in the basement?

You can bring chilled wine back to room temperature without harm. What wine doesn't like is exposure to sun.

Some recipes call for white wine. Does it matter which one I use?

When recipes call for white wine, they usually mean a dry white wine (as opposed to a sweet white or rosé.) A dry Chardonnay or Sauvignon Blanc will do fine. The wine needn't be expensive—a good white table wine will do. When you cook wine, the alcohol will burn off, leaving behind the wine's flavor.

How is it that Gewürztraminer has more alcohol in it than, say, a Chardonnay?

The Gewürztraminer grape grows in a cooler climate than the Chardonnay and so it needs to stay on the vine longer to ripen, resulting in a higher sugar content than the Chardonnay. The more sugar in a grape, the greater the alcohol content in the wine.

White ranges from very dry to sweet. (If you're confused, think of home-made lemonade which can be very tart to sweet, depending on the amount of sugar and lemons used.) Here's a chart to show you where the white varietals fall.

VERY DRY	DRY	MEDIUM-DRY
Sauvignon blanc	Chardonnay	Riesling
Tocai Friulano	Pinot Blanc	Gewürtztraminer
Viognier	Sémillon	
Melon de Bourgogne		
Pinot Gris (Pinot Grigio)		

HELPFUL RESOURCES

BOOKS

The Wall Street Journal Guide to Wine
By Dorothy J. Gaiter and John Brecher
Broadway Books

Hugh Johnson's How to Enjoy Your Wine
By Hugh Johnson
Simon & Schuster

3

Red Grape *varieties*

about red grape varieties

Turning red all over

What is it about red wine? It immediately conjures up scenes of rich, hearty meals around wooden tables in paneled rooms. This makes sense because most red wines are so full-bodied and flavorful. They are the perfect match for a savory cheese, a great steak, or a robust red pasta dish. And yes, reds are probably drunk more in cooler weather than the lighter white wines.

So why are reds so flavorful? Well, there are a number of reasons, the foremost being **tannin**—a naturally occurring substance found in the skins, seeds, and stems of red grapes. It gives red wines their character. The skin of the red grape is always what gives it its color. It's what wakes up your tongue when you drink a glass of strong red wine. In fact, a red wine is called **firm** if it's high in tannin, or **soft** if it's low.

Among the red varietels, or red grape types, are: Cabernet Sauvignon, Merlot, Pinot Noir, Zinfandel, Gamay, Syrah, and Grenache. Some reds are made of 100 percent of the varietal; Beaujolais, for example, is made from 100 percent Gamay grapes. Most are not 100 percent but have other grapes blended in to give the wine richness or smoothness, or to add flavor, texture, and complexity. It all comes down to what the winemaker is trying to create. Depending on the country's wine regulations, a wine must be 75 to 85 percent of one varietal if it is to be classified as such.

ASK THE EXPERTS

Can drinking red wine really reduce heart disease?
Medical research shows that drinking two four-ounce glasses of red wine a day can cut the risk of coronary disease by as much as 50 percent. It was found that the tannins in red wine contain antioxidant properties that help decrease levels of "bad" cholesterol and raise the levels of "good" cholesterol.

cabernet sauvignon

*The king of
the reds*

Cabernet Sauvignon is the strong, flavorful, and plentiful grape that has been cultivated in the Bordeaux region of France for centuries. It is also a remarkably steady and consistent performer in many other regions of the world, including South America, Australia, South Africa, and California. A Cabernet Sauvignon wine can be 100 percent Cabernet Sauvignon or blended with other grapes to create a slightly different flavor. Whether blended or not, a "Cab" (as it is nicknamed) is almost always **complex** (lots of interesting layers of taste to it) and **full-bodied** (rich in texture and weight—the opposite of **thin**).

Classically, Cabernet Sauvignon is described as having the flavor of black currants or **cassis** (a liqueur made from black currants). Cab has substantial fruitiness, with berry and plum aromas in addition to the black currant. It often also has a degree of spiciness and occasionally herbaceous—that is, herblike, almost minty—aromas, and when aged in oak can have hints of vanilla, smoke, clove, cedar, and of course, oak. A good Cab is full-bodied, rich, complex, and intensely flavorful.

Cabernet Sauvignon is often blended with Merlot or other grapes. What makes the partnership successful is that Merlot, which is not as spicy as Cab, has softer tannins and less acid.

A cousin to Cabernet Sauvignon is **Cabernet Franc**, an even spicier varietal. Cabernet Franc is grown in the Saint-Emilion district of Bordeaux and is also frequently blended with Merlot. Today, more and more American winemakers are making Cabernet Franc-based reds.

PETER SELECTS

- **Sebastiani "Cask"**
  Cabernet Sauvignon
  (Sonoma, California) $16-$18

- **Chateau Meyney St. Estèphe**
  (Bordeaux, France) $25-$30

- **Beringer "Knights Valley"**
  Cabernet Sauvignon
  (Napa Valley, California) $25-$30

- **Humberto Canale Gran Reserva**
  Cabernet Sauvignon
  (Rio Negro, Argentina)
  $13-$16

- **Wolf Blass Yellow Label**
  Cabernet Sauvignon
  (South Australia) $13-$15

merlot

The prince of red

If the Cabernet Sauvignon is king, then Merlot could be considered the prince of red wine, for it is much softer and less tannic. In the 1990s, Merlot soared to popularity virtually throughout the world. The Merlot grape is grown extensively in Bordeaux, where it is used for Bordeaux blends; but it is also found in Italy, South Africa, Australia, Chile, California, Washington State, and on Long Island in New York State.

Merlot enjoys softer tannins than Cabernet and is more velvety on the palate. It comes in several styles and flavors. In Italy and California, it can make a fruit-intensive, easy-to-enjoy wine, which is often Merlot at its most popular. It also comes in a richer style—and boasts black cherry, red cherry, and oak flavors. Merlot can benefit from blending, with Cabernet's extra tannins giving the blend a bit of firmness. It's this blending that makes the red Bordeaux wines of France so sublime.

SK THE EXPERTS

Why is Merlot so popular right now?
Because it is softer than Cabernet, it can be more pleasant to drink on its own, without food. In addition, because there is so much more Merlot being produced, it is now usually less expensive than Cabernets.

What about the Merlots of Washington State?
They can be quite excellent. Did you notice that Peter Selects lists a Columbia Crest Merlot first?

pinot noir

The grand duke

Pinot Noir is the pride of French red Burgundy, and most wine experts believe that it competes with Cabernet Sauvignon for top honors as the world's greatest red wine grape. Pinot Noir is also admired for its complex flavors. The French reign supreme in their cultivation of Pinot Noir and it is the basis of most Champagnes. Although it can be very difficult to grow, under optimal soil and weather conditions the resulting wine can be velvety in texture, majestic in flavor, and extraordinary in bouquet.

In the United States, as in Burgundy, Pinot Noir grows best in cooler growing regions, such as the Willamette Valley in Oregon; Mendocino County, the Carneros region of Napa, the Russian River, Green Valley, and Pacific Coastal districts of Sonoma, Monterey's Santa Lucia Highlands and the Santa Maria Valley near Santa Barbara—all in California.

Pinot Noir is also a bit temperamental. In fact, many growers consider it to be the most fickle of all grapes to grow because of its sensitivity to environment and soil. But at its best, Pinot Noir is a wine with tremendous finesse and charm.

The best examples of Pinot Noir offer a sophisticated, rich fruit flavor, especially raspberry. The aroma can resemble dried roses, earth, tar, herbs, bark, mushrooms, cola, and spices. Pinot Noir can also be light, with simple herbal flavors. It is ideal when served with meats and poultry, such as veal or cornish hen.

Red Burgundy is also an ideal red wine to accompany virtually all varieties of wild game. And all styles of Pinot Noir are perfect with cheese.

FIRST PERSON DISASTER

Saved by Sangria

My ex-boyfriend and I had forged enough of a friendship that I invited him to an informal dinner party to meet my new man. My ex arrived with a jug of hideous red wine —confirming why we were no longer together. My new boyfriend saved the day. "This is great!" he said, "we can make sangria!" He then proceeded to pour the jug wine into a pitcher, dilute it with orange juice, and then add slices of lemon and orange. Everybody was happy!

—Marjorie O., Santa Cruz, California

zinfandel

The quintessential California red

Possibly because of its vivid flavors and spicy, full-bodied charm, Zinfandel is considered to be the quintessential California wine. It is the most widely planted red grape in the state (although Merlot is sneaking up), and it is tremendously versatile. On its own it makes a sociable, full-bodied, flavorful red, a sweetish but popular rosé (known as White Zinfandel.) In inexpensive jug wines, it is commonly used for blending with other grapes, including Cabernet Sauvignon.

Thought to have originally come from Southern Italy, it has been one of California's great successes. Zinfandel is a challenging grape to grow. Its berry size varies significantly within a bunch, and therefore it ripens unevenly. As a result, it often needs to stay on the vine longer, resulting in sweeter juice and slightly higher alcohol.

Zinfandel has a number of flavors, sometimes depending upon its style. Normally berrylike, it boasts raspberry, blackberry, black cherry, and plum flavors, together with shades of tobacco, cedar, vanilla, and oak.

PETER SELECTS

- **Rabbit Ridge Barrel Cuvée**
  (California) $10-$12

- **Gallo Sonoma Stefani Ranch**
  (Sonoma, California)
  $18-$20

- **Ridge Sonoma Station**
  (Sonoma, California)
  $20-$25

- **Villa Mt. Eden Monte Rosso Vineyard**
  (Sonoma, California)
  $22-$25

gamay

The personable youth from Beaujolais

The Gamay grape is famous for the wines of France's Beaujolais region. Unlike many red wines, wines from Gamay grapes are better when drunk **young**—right after they are bottled. To many they are best known as Beaujolais Nouveau, a light red wine that appears on the shelf as soon after harvesting as possible, usually within six weeks. All Beaujolais is made from Gamay.

Gamay grapes produce light, fresh, fruity wines, often with strawberry or raspberry flavors. The grape is high in acidity and low in alcohol and very low in tannins. Its light taste makes it ideal to serve with fish, chicken, salads, and light luncheon dishes such as sandwiches, and light pastas.

PETER SELECTS

- **Beaujolais Nouveau Georges Duboeuf,** (Beaujolais, France) $6-$9

- **Brouilly Chateau de la Chaize** (Beaujolais, France) $9-$12

- **Moulin-a-Vent Joseph Drouhin** (Beaujolais, France) $15-$20

ALSO KNOWN AS

A variety of grape called Gamay is cultivated in California. Despite its name, it should not be confused with the French Gamays; in fact it is a clone of Pinot Noir. The Gamay grapes cultivated in California are known as Napa Gamay.

syrah/shiraz

What's old is new again

PETER SELECTS

● **Rosemount Diamond Table Shiraz**
(South Australia) $11–$13

● **Stonehaven Limestone Coast Shiraz**
(Australia) $15–$17

● **Crozes-Hermitage "Thalabert" Paul Jaboulet**
(Rhône Valley, France)
$24–$27

● **Renwood Syrah**
(Amador County, California)
$22–$27

One of the oldest recorded grape varieties is the Syrah. It harks all the way back to early Persia. To this day, it is a key blending grape. (It is Syrah that anchors the Rhône's world-famous Châteauneuf-du-Pape. See page 99.) Syrah is a relatively easy grape to grow and can also be found in other regions of France as well as California and Australia. In Australia, where it is known as Shiraz, it is more berrylike than the French-grown Syrahs. Austrialian Shirazes are often blended with Cabernet. While Syrah continues to be used as a blending grape in France, it is fast becoming a popular varietal wine on its own.

A deeply colored, powerful, long-lived wine, Syrah boasts pepper, spice, black cherry, tar, leather, and roasted nut flavors. It has a rich, smooth, supple texture and smooth, even tannins. It makes a great accompaniment to hearty, full-flavored food such as steak, and lamb or beef stews. It is also wonderful with game (deer, goose, and duck,) and strong cheeses, such as Roquefort and Stilton.

grenache

*The Spanish
grand duke*

An old Spanish variety, today Grenache is most often associated with the Côtes du Rhone wines of the Rhône Valley of France, where, like Syrah, it often serves as a blending wine to a number of truly superb wines. Grenache is grown throughout the world, especially in Spain, where it serves as part of the Spanish Rioja blend.

Grenache makes for full-bodied, fruity rosés and reds with a distinctive orange or bronze hue and berrylike flavors. Rioja—Spain's best known and finest red wine—is a blend of Grenache and another famous Spanish grape, Tempranillo.

In Spain, good red wine is traditionally served with grilled beef or pork, roasted lamb, cured ham, chorizo sausages, and tapas (spicy appetizers or snacks).

other red varietals

The following varietal reds are not as well known as their sisters but definitely deserve attention. Moreover, you may see them listed on the back of some bottles of blended wine.

Nebbiolo

Considered by many experts to be the great grape of northern Italy, Nebbiolo is at its best in rich, strong wines, particularly Barolo and Barbaresco, which are made entirely of Nebbiolo grapes. The wines are full-bodied and robust, high in tannin and alcohol. The flavors are rich, with hints of tar, strawberries, flowers, and truffles. These wines age very well and may need as many as 10 years to assume proper character. This grape grows best in Italy, but it is also being cultivated in California.

PETER SELECTS
- **Barolo, Marchese de Barolo** (Italy) $37-$40

Sangiovese

Sangiovese is best known for providing the backbone to many superb Italian red wines, including Chianti. It is just beginning to be grown in California and to take its place among popular wines on restaurant menus. It is medium- to full-bodied, has a supple "warm" texture, and boasts the flavors of raspberry, cherry, spices, and occasionally anise.

PETER SELECTS
- **Chianti Classico Aziano Ruffino** (Tuscany, Italy) $11-$12
- **Swanson Vineyards Sangiovese** (Napa Valley, California) $24-$28

Barbera

Grown primarily in Italy as well as California, Barberas can be rich, fruit-intensive wines that are relatively low in tannin but high in acidity. In California, Barberas are grown in warm regions and, like the Italian wines, are fruit-filled and soft.

- **Barbera d'Asti Michele Chiarlo**
  (Piedmont, Italy) $11-$13
- **Renwood Barbera**
  (Amador County, California) $19-$22

Tempranillo

Tempranillo is a major contributor to Spanish red wine. Indigenous to the country and rarely grown elsewhere, it is the dominating grape in two of Spain's most important wines: Rioja and Ribera del Duero. Usually dark garnet-colored, it often has hints of tea, brown sugar, vanilla, plums, tobacco, and cassis. A medium-bodied wine, it frequently has more acidity than tannin.

- **Sonsierra Tempranillo**
  (Rioja, Spain) $9-$10

Mourvèdre

Mourvèdre is a key red grape used in many Spanish wines. Increasingly popular, Mourvèdre wine tends to be high in tannin, with a fruit-intensive, often blackberry, flavor, although it can occasionally be somewhat gamey. Often blended with its Spanish relation, Grenache, Mourvèdre vines are also grown in Provence, Australia, and California.

- **Reserve St. Martin Mourvèdre**
  (Southwest, France) $7-$9

Malbec

The Malbec grape is responsible for many of Argentina's best wines. The hot, dry climate of Argentina's wine-growing regions is ideal for this not-too-hardy grape. Malbec wine is big, spicy, luxurious, and fruit-intensive, sometimes quite tannic. Some call it an "unpolished" red, but Argentine Malbecs are grand. Malbec is also grown in California, although it is still used there only as a blending grape.

- **Trapiche Oak Cask Malbec**
  (Mendoza, Argentina) $9-$10

answers to common questions

How long will an open bottle of red wine last? If I refrigerate it, will it last longer?

The minute you open a bottle of wine, it becomes exposed to air, which works its way into the wine and can cause a wine to turn sour in a few days. Refrigerating it will extend its life a few more days. Let it reach room temperature before serving.

What reds go well with pasta?

When choosing a wine to go with pasta, take your cue from the main ingredients in the sauce. For example, nothing goes better with a meaty Bolognese sauce than a red like Chianti. A quattro frommagi (four cheeses) calls for a Tuscan Sangiovese. If the pasta sauce is light, go with a white.

I saw an enormous bottle of wine at a reception. What is it called?

Oversized bottles of wine come in various sizes, each with its own name. A **magnum** holds 1.5 liters, the equivalent of two ordinary wine bottles. A **jeroboam** holds the equivalent of four regular bottles of wine or two bottles of champagne. A **rehoboam** holds 4.5 liters, or six regular bottles. A **methuselah** is the same as 8 standard bottles. And, finally, a **nebuchadnezzer** holds 15 liters or the equivalent of 20 standard bottles.

Red wine is often categorized by its style (or texture), which ranges from light to full-bodied. (If you're confused, think of milk, which can be skim, 2 percent or whole.) Light wines are typically low in alcohol and tannin, while full or heavy-bodied wines are usually high in alcohol content and tannins. Medium falls in between. Here's a chart to show you where the red varietals fall.

LIGHT-BODIED	MEDIUM-BODIED	FULL-BODIED
Gamay	Pinot Noir	Cabernet Sauvignon
Bardolino	Tempranillo	Cabernet Franc
	Sangiovese	Syrah (Shiraz)
	Barbera	Nebbiolo
	Merlot	Mourvedre
	Malbec	
Grenache	Zinfandel	

HELPFUL RESOURCES

WEB SITES

dailywine.com
Reviews and tasting notes on thousands of wines.

winetoday.com
Wine web site of The New York Times. Articles, reviews, and general information.

4

Before You Buy

FRUITY

HERBAL

EARTHY

SPICY

what's in a name

Is it the grape or the region?

Walking into a wine store can be a bit overwhelming. Mercifully, the reds and whites are usually separated. After that, however, you are on your own. Here's the first thing you need to know: wines are grouped in two ways—either by the variety of the grape, for example Chardonnay, or by the place or region where the grapes were grown and the wine was produced, such as California.

Wines named for their grape variety are called **varietal** wines. The two most popular grape varietals are the white Chardonnay and the red Cabernet Sauvignon. To keep the wine labels honest and meaningful, most wine-producing countries have an **appellation** or wine-categorization system that, among other things, sets out the minimum percentage of the grape variety that a varietal wine must contain in order to be called by that grape's name.

Vintage—or the year a wine is made—is another thing that confuses most people before they buy. Is there a difference between a 1995 bottle of Cabernet Sauvignon and a 1998? The answer lies in the quality of the grape harvests in those years. Grapes, just like anything else in nature, are subject to its whims. Droughts, pests, little sun, and lots of rain can all affect the taste of the wine. A good year that produces a plentiful harvest of excellent grapes is praised as a top **vintage** year. Wine experts keep tabs on each year and rate how each varietal from each region fared. These are called **vintage charts**. Most wine stores keep a chart handy.

Wine buffs often toss around the French concept of **terroir** (pronounced ter-wahr). All it means is the unique combination of each vineyard's natural factors: soil, climate, altitude, length of seasons, and even the slope of its hill. Changing these characteristics can produce strikingly different wines from the same grape variety (just as coffee beans grown in Colombia will taste very different from those grown in Kenya or Hawaii).

FIRST PERSON DISASTER

Is it a Chardonnay
or Is it a Chardonnay?

Bob and I had only been going out for about for a year, so I was thrilled when he invited me to dinner with his parents at a fancy restaurant in Boston. I wanted to impress Bob's dad—a wine afficionado—with my "knowledge," so when the maitre d' asked me if I wanted a glass of Chardonnay as a pre-dinner drink, I said, "Oh, no; I don't really like Chardonnay."

Worried that I had said something stupid, I tried to recoup by ordering a glass of Pouilly-Fuissé—something that I thought sounded cosmopolitan and French. Then Bob's dad said: "Oh, you might not like that one, honey! Pouilly-Fuissé is 100 percent French Chardonnay."

Awkwardly, I explained that I knew nothing about wine. Bob's dad suggested that I go ahead and try the Pouilly-Fuissé. Sure enough, it was fabulous wine. Bob and I have been married for eight years, and his dad sends us Pouilly-Fuissé for every anniversary.

—Sally Ann, Boston, Massachusetts

SK THE EXPERTS

Why is a jug bottle of Chablis from California so much cheaper than a bottle of French Chablis?

Jug wine is not about quality but quantity. To make their jug wine sound classier, some winemakers "borrowed" the name of the French region, Chablis. In France, Chablis wine is made from 100 percent Chardonnay grapes. Not so in the U.S. In fact, makers of white jug wine can use any grapes they want to make their wine and call it Chablis. So now American-made Chablis has come to stand for any cheap white wine.

What is the best way to store wine?

Ideally, wine bottles should be stored lying on their sides, so the wine is in touch with the cork. If a wine bottle stands for too long, the cork will dry out and air may leak into the bottle—interacting with the wine, changing its taste, and eventually turning it into vinegar. Also, for best results, store your wine in a dark, cool place, such as the basement or inside a cabinet.

How long will an open bottle of wine last?

If you cork it up tightly after you've opened it, it should last a day or two, perhaps three. What turns wine into vinegar is oxygen. The more oxygen there is in the bottle, the faster it will turn. A bottle with just a few ounces left will turn very quickly. A new device on the market called a Vacu Vin Wine Saver removes the oxygen in an open bottle and seals it with a reusable rubber cork to prolong the shelf life of wine for up to ten days.

Notes on Reading a Wine Label

Reading the fine print

Wine labels, like those on other food packages, provide technically accurate information about the contents. They can't, however, answer the most important question: Will you like it? At least they can help narrow down the choices.

A wine label will not necessarily show all the elements listed below but will almost always show the country of origin and the winery.

Country of origin: The country that produced the wine.

County or region: The locality that produced the wine. American wines may first list the state (for example, California) before the region (Napa Valley).

Vineyard: The winery.

Vintage: The year the grapes were grown, harvested, and made into this wine.

Appellation: The government-sanctioned locality designation that ensures minimum production standards.

Alcohol content: The amount of alcohol in the wine. Generally it is twice the concentration of beer and a fraction that of distilled spirits.

Special terms: The expressions "Estate Bottled" or "Produced and Bottled by the Winery" mean that the winemaker took great care to create a distinctive wine by controlling the process from growing to bottling. Expressions such as "Reserve," "Barrel-Fermented," and "Cuvée" may sound good but have no fixed meaning and do not necessarily indicate that the wine is special.

vintage of the
wine—the year
the wine was
harvested and
bottled

name of
winemaker
or producer

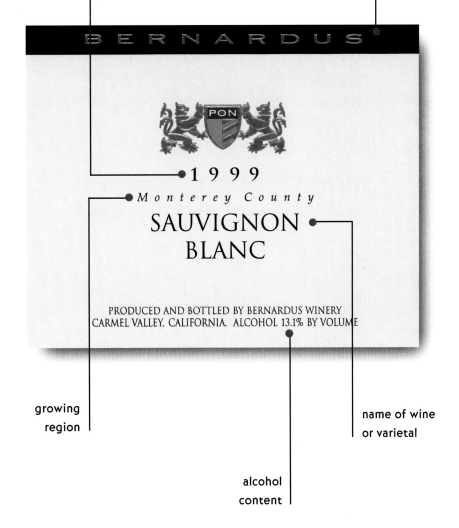

BERNARDUS

1999

Monterey County

SAUVIGNON
BLANC

PRODUCED AND BOTTLED BY BERNARDUS WINERY
CARMEL VALLEY, CALIFORNIA. ALCOHOL 13.1% BY VOLUME

growing
region

name of wine
or varietal

alcohol
content

about wine bottles and glasses

What to look for

The shape of the wine bottle can tell you right off what kind of wine you are dealing with. As you see in the boxes on the following pages, a Cabernet or Merlot wine bottle from Bordeaux or elsewhere has a distinctive shape, what winemakers call **high-shouldered**. Now take a look at a bottle of French Beaujolais, red Burgundy, American Pinot Noir, or Chardonnay. They traditionally come in **slope-shouldered** bottles. (Tall, skinny bottles, not shown here, are used for Riesling wines (see page 33).

Believe it or not, the shape and size of your wineglass can have a bit of an impact on how a wine tastes. As a result, wineglasses come in a variety of sizes and shapes. The most important thing when choosing a wineglass is that it be designed to show off the aromas of the wine when you smell it. A long stem is preferable so that, in holding it, your hand is at a distance from the bowl. Hands carry scents that might obscure those of the wine.

The rim of the wineglass curves in slightly for two reasons: to capture the aroma and prevent spills when swirling wine. (See tasting wine on page 71.) The glass should also be clear, not colored, to better view the subtleties of color in the wine. Although specially shaped glasses can enhance appreciation of certain wines, such as dessert wines, an all-purpose glass with a long stem and a 12-ounce capacity should work for regular use. Traditionally, white wine is served in smaller glasses, and Sherry, Port, and Madeira in even smaller ones. The narrowness of the champagne glass, called the flute, serves to focus the subtle aromas and show off the tiny bubbles. It holds about six ounces of champagne.

Ask THE EXPERTS

Is it necessary to invest in an expensive set of crystal?
Absolutely not! Certainly beautiful crystal wineglasses are marvelous, and an exquisite glass may, in fact, enhance your sensory experience; but a good, appropriately designed glass is all that is really necessary to appreciate good wine.

How do you care for a wineglass?
Wineglasses are fragile, so handle them carefully to avoid breakage. Just as important, keep them clean. Rewash prior to use and rinse thoroughly. Smell the glass, and make sure it does not smell like detergent or you will taste it in your wine. To eliminate this detergent smell, carefully coat the inside of the glass with the wine when you're pouring it.

Burgundy Bottle

A large bottle with sloping shoulders, a shortish neck and a deep punt (indentation in the bottom of the bottle). Used for both red and white wines, and in regions all over the world.

Burgundy Glass

An extra-large, apple-shaped bowl includes a large opening specially designed to capture the bouquet and aromas of a good Burgundy. Generally a 12- to 16-ounce capacity.

Bordeaux Glass

A bit smaller, and less bulbous than the Burgundy glass. The smaller opening captures the delicate quality of the Bordeaux. A good choice for an all-purpose wineglass.

Bordeaux Bottle

Often used for red wines that have to be laid down to age. Usually dark green with high shoulders—that is, they are more squared than sloping.

Choosing the right glass for the right wine

Champagne glass

Either a tulip-shaped glass or a trumpet-shaped flute, tall and narrow, that can be filled to the top. (Swirling isn't usually necessary since champagne bubbles exude the wine's flavor.)

Sparkling Wine Bottles

Extra-thick glass to hold in the pressure from carbonation. Can be dark green, dark brown, or even black with a high punt (the indentation in the bottom of the bottle).

Fortified Wine Glasses

Port is served in a small, elongated, tulip-shaped glass with a small opening. A sherry glass, called a copita, has a similar shape but is slightly smaller.

Port Bottles

Port bottles are always dark brown, have high shoulders like the Bordeaux bottles, and have a long, shaped neck in order to accommodate a larger cork.

Talking About Wine

A language of its own

Winetasting, like any other art, has its own unique vocabulary. Before you take a sip and try to talk the talk, you need to know what key wine terms mean. Here are some basic terms you'll hear when you taste wines.

Acidity All wines contain acid, but some wines are more acidic than others. Acidity is an important factor in white wines; it gives the wine crispness.

Balance Balance is the relationship among the four basic components in a wine: fruit, acidity, tannin, and alcohol. Tannin, alcohol, and acidity firm up a wine. Fruit softens it.

Body The impression of a wine's size and weight is expressed as full-bodied or light-bodied. Certain reds, for example, Bordeaux or Barolo, seem fuller, bigger, or heavier in the mouth than lighter reds, such as a Beaujolais .

Bouquet A wine's aroma. The word "smell" is rarely used to describe wine. Sometimes the word "nose" is used.

Complexity The different flavors and textures that you taste in a wine. The more the better. A straightforward wine is fine, but a complex wine is invariably better quality.

Depth A measure of complexity. Depth is used to describe a wine that is not flat but multidimensional, with many layers of taste.

Dry In wine lingo, dry is the opposite of sweet.

Length A second measure of complexity. The wine hits all the taste centers on your tongue and lingers after you swallow. Also known as a good finish. In contrast, a "short" wine may make a big impression when it comes into the mouth, but is lost almost immediately. Length is a sign of a quality wine.

Nose Like bouquet, a description of a wine's aroma. A wine with a "huge nose" has a strong scent.

Palate The flavor of the wine, specifically, the impression that the wine gives when in your mouth, such as smooth, hearty, or light.

Sweetness The opposite of sweet is dry.

Tannin A natural acid in grape skins and stems and in oak barrels used for aging. Because reds are fermented with their skins, tannin levels are far higher in red wines than in white wines.

Texture Just as your mouth can perceive hot and cold, sweetness and tartness, it can also perceive texture. Some wines feel "soft" and "smooth" while others seem "rough" or "coarse."

Typical A term that experts use to describe how "typical" a wine is to its soil, vintage, and grape variety. You need years of tasting to acquire the experience to recognize this—but at least getting there requires drinking lots of wine!

FLAVORFUL DESCRIPTIONS

Listen to some people describe a wine and it sounds as if they spend most of their time in gardens and kitchens. That is because wines do remind people of certain fruits, foods, and spices. These flavors have not been added to the wine, but created by the winemaker's skill in fermenting the grape. They get grouped as:

Floral: Dried roses, honeysuckle, spring flowers, violets
Fruit: Berries, cherries, plum, apple, citrus, or apricot
Earth: Mushrooms, forest, or dry leaves
Spice: Cinnamon, cloves, or pepper
Herb: Mint, grass, hay, rosemary

how to taste wine

Tasting wine—as opposed to simply drinking it down, means taking the time to judge its qualities. It can conjure up intimidating visions of wine snobs sitting in judgment, not of the wine but of you. Can't tell the difference between a cheap Chianti and an expensive Bordeaux? Don't fret; tasting is the only way to learn how. Keep the wine snobs out of your mind by focusing on the three elements in tasting wine: appearance, aroma, and flavor.

Appearance. How does the wine look in the glass? Regardless of whether the wine is red or white, is it dark or pale? Swirl the wine in the glass. Does it all slide down into the glass or does it leave a few spikey trails behind? If it leaves trails of wine, it's a plus. It means the wine is rich in body. Wine experts call this having good **legs**.

Aroma. Your sense of smell, if properly used, can greatly enhance your tasting of a wine. So put your nose to work and rotate the glass so that the wine swirls inside the glass, mixing with the air. Bring the glass to your nose quickly, and put your nose into the glass as far as it will go without actually touching the wine. Smell. Is the aroma fruity? Fresh? Intense? In any case, the aroma should be pleasant. If it smells "skunky" or "corked," send it back or open another bottle.

Taste. After you have looked at and smelled the wine, take a sip. (See below.) Swish the wine around in your mouth as if you are chewing. Then swallow. You should be able to taste several things with the wine. The first thing your tongue will register is either dryness or sweetness, followed by acidity, fruit, and tannin. Then note whether the wine is heavy, light, smooth, or rough. Most wine flavors, however, take several seconds to taste because they are actually aromas vaporized in the mouth and perceived through the rear nasal passage rather than through the tastebuds on your tongue.

STEP BY STEP: TASTING WINE

1 Pour only two ounces into the glass.

2 Gently swirl it around so it coats the sides of the glass. Does it cling to the sides? Then it's got legs and will probably taste more full-bodied than those wines that simply slide quickly down the glass.

3 Put your nose inside the glass and inhale the aroma.

4 Take a sip . . . but don't swallow. Hold it in your mouth for a few seconds. Pay attention to which parts of your mouth are feeling the wine. Any puckering sensations at the back of the tongue and throat? That's the effect of tannin. Any prickling on the tongue? That's the wine's acidity coming through.

5 Take a little breath while it's still in your mouth to intensify the wine's flavor.

6 Swallow. Is there a finish?

7 Take another sip and see what other flavors you can discern.

answers to common questions

How do I tell which grape is in the wine?

Often it is on the label. If a grape variety (Merlot, or Chardonnay) is named on the label, then a minimum of 75 percent of that grape must make up that wine in the U.S. If the wine is European, the grape varietal will probably not be mentioned on the label; rather it will list the region where the grapes were grown. Don't be afraid to ask the wine store owner what type of grape varietal—or varietals if it's a blend— are used in the wine.

What does Appellation d'Origine Controlée mean?

Better known as the AOC, this is determined by a regulatory body in France that controls the amount of wine that can legally be produced from vineyards located in the region, district, or village designated on the label. Since where a wine is grown is key, on a French wine label the wine's place name is substituted for the word d'Origine, which is French for region of origin. For example, Appellation Bordeaux Controlée is a wine from the Bordeaux region.

Italy has a similar system, called Denominazione di Origine Controllata (DOC), as does the United States. The American system was adopted in 1978 and defines more than 100 American Viticulture Areas (AVAs).

What factors determine the quality of a wine, and are they reflected in the price?

Three factors determine if a wine is of good character: 1. the vintage; 2. the climate and soil, or **terroir,** where the grapes are cultivated; and 3. the winemaker's skill and objective. The price may or may not reflect these things.

Are there publications that rate wine?

Yes. *The Wine Spectator*, a magazine that is published every two weeks, rates wine, as does *The Wine Advocate*, a newsletter on wine. Both use a 100-point grading system, with 100 the top score. Wines are sometimes tasted blind (meaning the wine's label is hidden). Tasters rate wine on numerous factors, such as appearance, bouquet, flavor, balance, and finish. An excellent wine rates between 90 and 100; a good wine rates 80 to 89; and 70 to 79 is average to below average. Anything under 70, forget it.

HELPFUL RESOURCES

MAGAZINES

The Wine Spectator

This glamorous magazine is published every two weeks and supplies extensive coverage of all international wine regions as well as tasting notes. For subscription information, call: 800-752-7799

The Wine Enthusiast

Staff written with extensive wine-buying notes, this magazine is published monthly. For subscription information, call: 800-356-8466

WEB SITES

WineSpectator.com

In association with The Wine Spectator *magazine, this is an excellent source of information on wine.*

WineEnthusiast.com

Great source for wine accessories, plus articles and wine reviews from The Wine Enthusiast *magazine.*

5

Buying Wine *101*

wine stores

*What to expect
from your local
wine shop*

The best wine stores specialize in wine. The owners study it and try to taste as many wines as possible before they buy. Of course, most liquor stores sell wine, but they are usually not wine shops. The owner of a traditional liquor store is not necessarily a wine expert, nor should you expect him or her to be. The owners of wine stores are precisely that: people who specialize in selling wines and can help you make the right selection.

Mystified as to how wine stores work? Most wine stores organize and display their wines according to country of origin (France, Italy, the United States), and then break the countries down by region (Bordeaux in France; Piedmont in Italy; Napa Valley in California). Within these breakdowns, wines are organized by color (red or white) or varietal (e.g., Merlot or Chardonnay).

There are often special sections for Champagne and sparkling wines, fortified wines, and dessert wines. A good shop may also

76

have a locked cabinet, or perhaps even a special refrigerated room, for fine wines. Nearly all wine stores sell the amenities of wine: corkscrews, ice buckets, and other extras.

What are the signs of a good wine store? First of all, a cool temperature. Wines like a consistent climate of 65 degrees F. (Wine bottles that have marks or drips around the cork or label have been overheated. Don't buy them.) While there may be one or two bottles standing for easy viewing, the majority should be stored lying flat in racks. All bottles should be kept out of direct sunlight.

SK THE EXPERTS

I'm still anxious about buying wine in a shop. What can I do to make it easier?
Ask yourself these four questions before you walk in: Why am I buying wine (for a casual supper or special occasion)? How much money do I want to spend? What (if any) food will be served with this wine? What style of wine do I want (red, white, dry, sweet, etc.)? Based on your answers, a good wine store owner should be able to help you find the perfect wine.

Don't wine stores tend to have higher prices than liquor stores?
No. Moreover, a wine store will have a much greater selection to chose from, as well as a knowledgeable staff. That said, there are no set retail prices for wine. It is up to the store owner's discretion.

Can I get a discount if I buy a lot?
Very often you can, since wine merchants are naturally keen on customers who buy a lot. If you buy a case of wine (12 bottles), most wine stores offer a 10 percent discount off the total price.

What if the wine tastes bad?
Return it. You should get your money back, or at the very least a new bottle.

wine superstores and other outlets

More wine, less expertise

Buying from a fine wine merchant used to be the only way to purchase good wine. Today, however, fine wine can be found in some discount chain stores and upscale supermarkets, some of which offer a surprisingly dazzling selection.

Bear in mind, however, that although some "wine superstores" may appear to have a broader selection than your local vintner, they may simply have more bottles of wine—not more types. It's a bit like those huge office supplies stores, where they have rows and rows of copy paper instead of the one row your local stationery store has. What's more, superstores usually don't have the very special wines. They're designed to have the most popular wines at good prices. Also, the clerks in superstores are usually not trained, nor are they knowledgeable about wine. They will be able to tell you where to find the Champagne, but they probably won't know which one is the best, let alone why.

If you plan on shopping at a wine superstore, don't be overwhelmed by the sheer volume of bottles. Prepare ahead of time and have a list of two or three wines you know you want.

In some states, such as California, wine is also sold in supermarkets, along with food and household products. Usually, these supermarket wines are rather ordinary, and include the large jug wines and less expensive generic wines.

Wine is being sold in many other places these days. Ads with toll-free numbers in newspapers and magazines offer wine at supposedly good prices. Many retailers publish catalogs, especially during the Christmas holidays, offering hundreds of wines and gift packages. Wine-of-the-month clubs also offer many ideas.

FIRST PERSON DISASTER

Julia, Forgive Me!

I had just discovered Julia Child's *Mastering the Art of French Cooking*, and began experimenting. It was such fun. When I was finally ready to show off my new-found culinary skills, my husband and I invited some close friends over for dinner. I worked all day making Julia's traditional coq au vin—chicken cooked in a savory red wine sauce.

We were living on a tight budget, but I went all out on the ingredients: the best chicken, the freshest vegetables. Unfor-tunately, I thought it didn't matter what kind of wine I used in the recipe, as it would be cooked off. I found a dusty bottle of red something-or-other for $1.99 in the grocery store and used it. I didn't notice anything strange while the chicken was cooking, but with the first bite, I knew it was "off." Hardly anyone ate their chicken, ruined by the lousy wine. Never again would I scrimp on "cooking" wine!

— Pam T., New York, New York

wine in a restaurant

*Remember,
it's all about
marketing*

A certain amount of ritual and romance has grown up around wine, particularly when savoring it in a restaurant. To many, however, selecting wine can be an intimidating experience. Maybe that's because wine in restaurants is big business with mark-ups ranging from 200 to 500 percent.

Fortunately, most restaurants follow the same pattern when listing the wines they offer (see pages 82-83 for an example). Typically, the wines are listed first by color (red or white), then either by varietal (Cabernet Sauvignon, Merlot) or by country and region of origin (French Bordeaux wines; Californian wines). Within these groupings, they are usually ranked by price, with the least expensive at the top of the listing and the most expensive at the bottom. Good wine lists also include half bottles, which hold about three glasses of wine.

Many restaurants offer "house wines," at least one, and often several, white and red. If you order a glass of house wine for an **aperitif,** or pre-dinner drink, and like it, you might want to order a half carafe, which should allow about three glasses. Better restaurants may have four or five different reds or whites to choose from. Ordering wine by the glass is a terrific way to experiment with different wines.

SK THE EXPERTS

What should I do when a waiter presents a bottle?

First, check that this is the wine that you ordered. The waiter will then place the cork in front of you to check that it is in one piece and not dried out. (A damaged cork may indicate that air has gotten into the wine and possibly spoiled it.) You can even smell it to make sure it is not "corky" or unpleasant. Finally, he or she will pour a bit of wine into your glass. Sniff it and take a small sip. (See page 69 for tasting techniques.) If it tastes the way it should, say, "It's fine," or give some indication that all is well. The server will pour for all others at the table, finishing with you.

What if the wine tastes bad?

If the wine smells skunky, corked, or tastes bad, tell the server immediately, before the others are served, and describe what doesn't seem right. In most good restaurants, the server will take you at your word and give you a new bottle. If the server argues that the wine is fine, ask to speak with the owner, and remind him or her that the customer is always right.

What's a sommelier?

A **sommelier** (pronouced som-mel-yay) is the proper name for the restaurant's resident wine expert. They are highly trained, and usually put together the establishment's wine list. Only the very best restaurants have a sommelier on staff. Most restaurants leave the taking of wine orders up to the maitre d' or the owner, either of whom should be able to help you with the wine list.

the wine list

Here's a sample wine list. It divides the wine into reds and whites, then lists them by their grape varietal (e.g. Merlot, Chardonnay). The name of the winemaker identifies each wine, then the region and the year the wine was made.

Vin Rouge —Red Wine Selection

Varietals

Chateau Robin, Côtes de Castillon, 1997

Winemaker	District	Vintage

● <u>Vin de Bordeaux</u>

Chateau Robin, Côtes de Castillon, 1997	
Chateau Cambon la Pelouse Haut Medoc Cru Bourgeois, 1996	32
Chateau Leloup, Saint Emilion Grand Cru, 1996	36
Chateau Paran Justice, St Emilion Grand Cru, 1996	40
Chateau Haut Surget, Lalande Pomerol, 1997	44
Chateau Ramage De La Batisse, Haut Medoc, 1995	48
Chateau Latour Du Pin Figeac, Grand Cru, Saint Emilion, 1997	62

● <u>Merlot</u>

Seven Peaks (Central Coast), 1998	32
Estancia, (Alexander Valley) 1997	36
Sebastiani (Sonoma Country), 1996	38
Kenwood, Jack London Vineyard (Sonoma), 1997	56
St. Clement, Napa Valley 1996	57

● <u>Cabernet Sauvignon</u>

Durney Vineyards (**Carmel Valley**), 1995	28
Los Vascos Domaines Barons De Rothchild (Lafite), 1998	28
Chateau Ste. Michelle (Washington), 1997	30
Foppiano Vineyards (Russian River Valley), 1998	40
Bernardus Marinus Meritage, (Carmel Valley), 1996	75

Vin Blanc — White Wine Selection

Varietals

● Sauvignon Blanc, Chenin Blanc

Bergerac Domaine de L'Houmme, 1998	28
Sancerre, La Chatellerie, 1999	32
Sauvignon Blanc, Chateau Potelle (Napa Valley) 1998	33
Vouvray, Champalou (Cuvée des Fondraux), 1998	35
Pouilly-Fume, Cuvée de Boisfleury, 1998	39
Pessac-Leognan, Grand Cru Classé, Chateau Carbonnieux, 1996	40

● Chardonnay, Vin de Bourgogne

Sonoma Cutrer (Russian River Ranches), 1999	36
Pouilly-Fuissé, **Morcel** Vincent, 1998	36
Chablis, Domaine de Bieville, 1997	36
Cambria (Santa Barbara), 1997	40
Steele (California), 1998	40

● Vin Rose

L'Alycastre, (Côtes de Provence) 1999	28

Champagne & Sparkling

Dom Perignon 1992	195
Moet et Chandon Brut Imperial NV	85
Veuve Clicquot Brut NV	79
Laurent Perrier Brut NV	75
Pommery Brut NV	70
Pacific Echo Brut NV	35

WINE BY THE GLASS

Pinot Grigio	*7*
Jamiesons Run, Shiraz, cabernet merlot	*8*
Chateau D'Hardouin, Merlot	*7*
Cellier Des Dauphins, Syrah	*6*
Chateau De Poce, Sauvignon Blanc	*7*
Domaine de L'Olivier, Chardonnay	*6*
Champagne Laurent Perrier	*12*

opening a bottle of wine

Cork—it can make or break a wine

Next to ordering wine in a restaurant, few things make people as nervous about wine as uncorking a bottle at home. Practice makes perfect. First, the tops of most wine bottles are covered with a piece of thin foil or plastic called a **capsule**. This needs to be removed before you can even get to the cork. Sometimes it peels off; sometimes you need to use a sharp knife to cut through it. (An inexpensive device called a "foil cutter" is available for precisely this purpose.)

Once you've managed to remove the foil, there's the cork. Enter the corkscrew. Corkscrews come in many varieties. The "waiter's corkscrew" or the "waiter's friend" looks a little bit like a big pocketknife with a lever, a little screw, and a small knife. It may be the most professional and perhaps the trickiest tool to use. The most popular one is the Screwpull—a very well-designed corkscrew that allows you to easily screw into the center of the cork, then simply continue to turn. The cork rises with no pulling or yanking.

Cork-sealed bottles of sparkling wine or champagne can be challenging to open. Not to belabor the obvious, but these corks don't require a corkscrew, you simply hold the cork still and twist the bottle to get the cork out. Before starting, point the bottle away from yourself and others in case the cork shoots out. Untie the metal wire, quickly cover the top with a cloth napkin held in your hand, then slowly turn the bottle, keeping your hand on the cork, as the pressure releases and the cork begins to push its way out. The napkin will be there in case the wine comes spewing out.

 **ASK THE EXPERTS**

Why are corks used to seal wine?
Cork, the soft and pliant bark of the cork tree, expands inside a bottle in order to keep the air out. (Air is wine's natural enemy. Exposure to air is what turns wine into vinegar.) Corks can be flawed (a rare occurrence) or dry out—both of which can affect a wine's taste. Moreover, dry corks can be problematic to remove, sometimes breaking in the process and leaving bits of cork floating in the wine.

What if the cork breaks and I can't get it all out?
The best solution is to use a chopstick or pencil and push the broken cork into the bottle. Before you pour the wine, get a small strainer and place it over your wineglass. Pour the wine through the strainer so it will catch the bits of cork before they land in your glass. Or if bits fall in the glass, you can simply fish them out. To restop the bottle, use any other cork.

Is it true that jug wines last longer than expensive wines once they're opened?
Yes. Jug wines will keep longer than expensive wines bcause they have been pasteurized and contain no microorganism that will cause the wine to turn bad after prolonged exposure to air.

answers to common questions

I usually see a handful of wines on sale at my local wine shop. Should I buy them?

Even the best shops have special sale wines, sometimes stacked at the front of the store. In a good wine shop, these sale items may well be worth your attention. The wine merchant wants your goodwill, so these wines most likely are not "bad" wines. Try a bottle to see if you like it, but don't buy a case of it just because it's on sale.

Can I buy wine over the Internet?

Yes . . . but whether you're legally able to receive it is another question. Each state in the U.S. controls the sale of alcohol within its borders. Some states, like New York, don't allow wine to be shipped directly to you from a Web site or from an out-of-state vineyard. Check your local regulations before ordering online.

What is a Wine Bar?

There is a new kind of restaurant around, designed to cater to wine lovers. It is called a wine bar and basically it's a theme restaurant where the theme is wine. Most serve lunch as well as dinner.

A good wine bar offers dozens or, in the case of Morrell Wine Bar & Café, in New York's Rockefeller Plaza, over 100 wines by the glass.

Wine bars offer the beginner and the expert a fun way to taste and enjoy wine without having to purchase the entire bottle.

HELPFUL RESOURCES

WEB SITES

Vine2wine.com
A central source that leads wine-loving Internet surfers to over 2,000 Web sites concerning wine.

Wineinstitute.org
The Web site of the Wine Institute, a public advocacy group of California wineries. Among other things, their site lists the laws governing the sales of wine for each state.

Can you have wine shipped home from a winery?

As a result of Prohibition's repeal, each state regulates the sale of alcohol as it sees fit. That has led to a patchwork of regulations for each state. Depending on where you live (see map below), a winery may or may not be able to ship wine to you. If you can't get the wine shipped directly, ask the winery what stores near your home sell their wine.

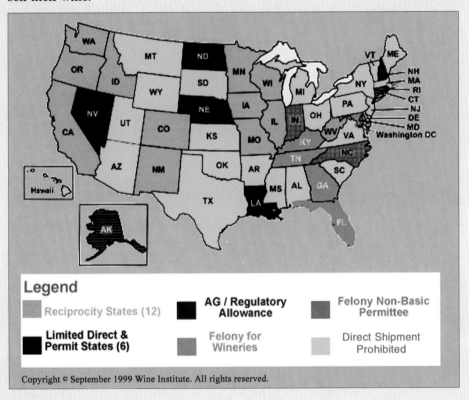

Legend

- Reciprocity States (12)
- **Limited Direct & Permit States (6)**
- **AG / Regulatory Allowance**
- Felony for Wineries
- Felony Non-Basic Permittee
- Direct Shipment Prohibited

6

French Wines

about french wines

*The world
standard
for hundreds
of years*

Although the French didn't invent wine, they perfected its production, so that by the early 18th Century French wine became the standard against which all other wines were judged. To maintain these standards and keep upstarts from stealing their better-known names, the French went one step further and created a set of regulations called **Appellation d'Origine Contrôlée** (AOC or AC) to ensure the quality of vineyard practices and the wines that result. All French wines are thus judged according to specific AOC regulations that take into account the following criteria: the quality of the land, the grapes, the amount grown, the alcohol content, and the way the wine is made.

Under French law, all French wine must be classified into one of four grades. Appellation d'Origine Contrôlée (AOC or AC) guarantees that the best French wines came from where they claim and were made according to the prescribed standards. On a wine label, the name for a region will be substituted for the words "d'Origine." For example, Appellation Bourgogne Contrôlée is a wine from the Burgundy **region** (Burgundy being the English spelling for the French Bourgogne region). The more specific the label gets, such as stating which district or specific vineyard within the region, the more select the wine is. These wines are considered the best.

A qualitatively lower level of wine is designated **Vin Délimité de Qualité Supérieure** (VDQS). **Vin de Pays** (literally, "country wine") identifies wines comparable to good California jug wines, and **Vin de Table** designates very ordinary table wine.

Within these four categories are levels of detail that take into account the various unique aspects of individual villages, districts, and regions. Only those vineyards whose wine has consistently made top grade can label their wine AOC, that is, to be known by the appellation, or name, of the wines of its growing area.

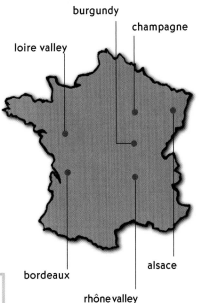

ASK THE EXPERTS

Why is France known more for its wine than Germany or Italy?
The reason is climate. Over centuries, France has identified particular areas whose soil and weather patterns produce particularly excellent quality wines. France also has a greater diversity of climates that range from the Champagne region in the north to the sunny Mediterranean coast. All of Germany's wine districts are as far north as France's northern Champagne and Alsace districts. Italy, on the other hand, is home to some wonderful reds, but its warmer climates make creating top-flight white wines difficult.

bordeaux

Prestige in a bottle

Bordeaux, a region in France, is famous for its rich, full-bodied, dry red wines. Cabernet Sauvignon (see page 44), Cabernet Franc (see page 44), and Merlot (see page 45) are Bordeaux's reigning grapes. From these grapes some of the best wines in the world have been created.

Bordeaux is home to some of the most celebrated vineyards in the world: Château Lafite-Rothschild, Château Margaux, and Château Latour to name but a few. (**Château** is the French word for castle, and has come to mean wine estate.) These wine estates have been making wines for hundreds of years and have elevated the science of making wine into an art. It doesn't come as a surprise that over a quarter of all first-class French AOC wines come from Bordeaux.

But in addition to their AOC ratings (see page 90), the best Bordeaux wines are classified under yet another system, begun in 1855. (Oh, those French!) Where the AOC guarantees the origin of a wine, this Bordeaux system grades each individual vineyard. It is called the **cru** classification (cru being the French word for growth). To this day, only five Bordeaux wineries have earned the first-rate status that lets them put the words **premier grand cru** on their labels. They are Château Lafite-Rothschild, Château Latour, Château Margaux, Château Haut-Brion, and Château Mouton-Rothschild. About 100 châteaux or wine estates that didn't make the top grade were classified Deuxième, Troisième, Quatrième, and Cinquième grand crus (second, third, fourth, and fifth great growths). Many good châteaux were rated **cru bourgeois**. Within the bourgeois grade there are several subcategories, such as superior and exceptional.

But don't get too caught up on the 1855 classification. There are many more delicious yet reasonably priced unclassified château wines from various districts in Bordeaux, including Saint-Émilion, Fronsac, Graves, and Côtes de Blaye. The best are soft, fruit-filled wines, with many made from Merlot grapes. Many châteaux located in Bordeaux's Medoc, Haut-Médoc, and Graves districts produce attractive, early maturing, yet unclassified Cabernet Sauvignon dominant wines. Although Bordeaux is most famous for its rich, full-bodied dry reds, it also produces dry white wines and sweet white wines, most notably Sauternes.

Château des Milles Anges

burgundy

*Home to
Clos de Vougeot,
Chablis, and
other world-
class wines*

Burgundy is another famous wine-producing region in France. An easy way to tell if a wine is from a Burgundy winery is that it uses the word **domaine** (for property) instead of **château** (estate) to refer to its vineyard. Also, while Bordeaux is primarily famous for its red wines, Burgundy boasts both exquisite reds and whites, many of which are among the finest wines in the world.

Red Burgundies are very different from their Bordeaux counterparts. Made from the Pinot Noir grape (as opposed to the Cabernet of Bordeaux), they are lighter in color, medium-to full-bodied, relatively low in tannin, and velvety on the palate. The flavors resemble cherries, raspberries, moss, wild mushrooms, and other woodsy tastes. With age, such well-known red Burgundies as Pommard, Volnay, and Beaune from the Côte de Beaune, and Nuits-Saint-Georges, Gevrey Chambertin, and Vosne-Romanée from the Côte de Nuits develop great complexity with extraordinary nuances of flavor and finesse. (Côte is the French word for slope.)

White Burgundies are made entirely from the Chardonnay grape and express a unique fullness of flavor, which includes hazelnuts and honey in a Meursault and floweriness and butterscotch in a Puligny-Montrachet or Chassagne-Montrachet. With age, the flavors develop even more complexity. Chardonnay from other regions can be good, but there's nothing quite like a great white Burgundy.

ASK THE EXPERTS

How long should a red Burgundy age?

A red Burgundy requires 3 to 10 years to mature, so plan on holding on to recent vintages for a while.

Why do some burgundy wines have their own AOC label?

The growing conditions in Burgundy's soil vary so dramatically that soil from two sites of the same vineyard can often produce wines different in style and quality. That's why the AOC structure for Burgundy includes tiers for individual vineyard sites of exceptional quality, called premier and grand crus.

Is expensive French Chablis really that much better than American Chablis?

You may have seen huge jugs labeled "Chablis" or "California Chablis" in your wine shop or local supermarket. This beverage bears absolutely no resemblance to the high quality of real Chablis, which is usually a fairly pricey wine beginning at $15 and going as high as $50 per bottle. This is an instance of you get what you pay for.

Why isn't French Chablis labeled as being from Burgundy?

Although Chablis is located in the northernmost part of Burgundy, it is considered a region of its own. That's why the wine labels say "Chablis" not "Bourgogne" (the French spelling of Burgundy).

beaujolais

*France's
paradise*

The Beaujolais district of France is the home of the red Gamay
grape (see page 49). You may be familiar with Beaujolais from
the annual news reports of the first consumption of Beaujolais
Nouveau—a red wine that appears in American wine shops about
six weeks after the harvesting of the grapes in France. It is fruity,
very low in tannins, and is a light, refreshing beverage that can be
drunk on its own or with dinner.

Beaujolais Nouveau appears in the United States near Thanksgiving,
which is perfect because it goes well with turkey and other fowl. It is
also good with pastas with pink and red sauces. It is also an ideal

wine for a number of lighter fares, such as sandwiches or a picnic of cold chicken. Keep in mind that Beaujolais Nouveau is at its best within six months of vintage. It is not meant to be aged.

Other Beaujolais wines, known as the **Crus Beaujolais**, hold up better to a little aging. These include Brouilly, Fleurie, Moulin-à-Vent, and Morgon.

There are several classifications of the Beaujolais region: Beaujolais, Beaujolais-Villages, and at the top, Cru Beaujolais. The wines of Beaujolais-Villages have slightly higher alcohol and are invariably of better quality than ordinary Beaujolais. The Crus of Beaujolais have still greater charm, fruit, and character.

FIRST PERSON DISASTER

Making a splash

My wife and I recently had a private tour of the world-famous Château Margaux, arranged by a friend in the wine industry. After the tour, we were taken into a private, very pristine tasting room. On the spotless white counter, we saw a bottle of red wine and three glasses, arranged with perfect precision. We felt as though we were standing on hallowed ground. Finally, a young woman wearing a long white lab coat entered. She gave a brief talk on the very special wine we were to taste, then removed the cork and partially filled our glasses. She continued talking, all the time aerating the wine by deftly swirling it around. Assuming this was a cue, I swirled too. A bit too enthusiastically, though, because no sooner had I started when the wine swirled right out of the glass and onto her white coat, the counter, and the floor. She kindly poured me another glass. The result of the winetasting? It was a superb wine, glorious in taste and hue, but its color was no redder than my face.

—Richard M., Vero Beach, Florida.

the rhône valley

A fascinating variety of robust reds

The Rhône Valley, located south of Burgundy, is home to the Grenache grape, a spicy red grape (see page 51). Grenache provides raspberry and herbal flavors, but often produces high alcohol content and low acidity. That's why Rhône winemakers often add Syrah and Mourvèdre grapes to balance their wines. Rhône wines are considered to be among the most robust and long-lived wines in all of France. These are big, hearty, food-friendly wines. A red wine from the Rhône is usually heartier and more full-bodied than a Cabernet Sauvignon. One of the most famous such reds comes from a region in the Rhône called Châteauneuf-du-Pape.

The Rhône River flows south, the northern portion passing the city of Lyon. This area produces little wine (only about 5 percent of the Rhône Valley's total production), making its wines relatively expensive. The northern Rhône makes spicy, full-bodied, dark red wines from such areas as Côte-Rôtie, Cornas, Hermitage, Saint Joseph, and Crozes-Hermitage.

The southern Rhône flows through a dusty plain, favorable to the Grenache grape that is the primary variety in the region's blended wines. The AOC appellations for the various regions that produce southern Rhône reds are: Côtes-du-Rhône, Côtes-du-Rhône-Villages, Vacqueyras, Gigondas, and Châteauneuf-du-Pape.

The Rhône Valley also produces some whites from Grenache Blanc, Marsanne, Rousanne, and the newly-celebrated Viognier variety. The voluptuous Rhône whites boast exotic peach, honey, nut, and honey-suckle flavors. Although Rhône whites are relatively rare, they are unmatched—and very expensive. Among the notable whites are those from Condrieu, Hermitage, and Châteauneuf-du-Pape vineyards.

CHÂTEAUNEUF-DU-PAPE
French history in a bottle

Châteauneuf-du-Pape is the most famous designated winegrowing region covered by AOC rules in the Rhône, and one of the most important in France. Aside from the fact that this region produces some remarkable red and white wines, its fame comes in part because it is huge. The region's vineyards extend over 7,500 acres.

Its name means "Pope's new castle" and came from the relocation of the Italian papal court to French Avignon in the 14th century. Pope Clement V from Gascony suppos-edly ordered the planting of vines, but it was his successor, Pope John XXII who developed the papal vineyard at Châteauneuf-du-Pape.

Châteauneuf-du-Pape produces a robust red wine, made from a blend of many grape varieties, primarily Grenache, Mourvèdre, and Syrah. At their best they are full-bodied, complex, flavor-intensive, long-lived, and high in alcohol. Châteauneuf-du-Pape's white wine is made from Grenache Blanc and Clairette grapes. It offers a full-bodied alternative to Chardonnay.

the loire valley

*A haven for
Sauvignon Blanc*

If the Rhône is known for full-bodied reds, the Loire is known for light, refreshing, relatively inexpensive whites. They all have remarkable acidity and vivid fresh-fruit flavors. The wines are rarely, if ever, fermented or stored in oak barrels. Rather, tradition holds that the wine be fermented in steel tanks. This means that almost all Loire wines don't have oaky overtones to them.

The Loire is France's longest river, running for more than 600 miles. Like the Rhône, it passes through several regions. The upper Loire Valley's cool climate and rolling hills produce some of the world's best Sauvignon Blanc grapes (see page 30). Sancerre and Pouilly-Fumé (not to be confused with the Chardonnay-based

Pouilly-Fuissé) are brisk white wines with citrus, steely, and grassy flavors. Sancerre tends to be fruitier, while Pouilly-Fumé is steely, dry, and more full-bodied. Both are usually best drunk young.

The mid-Loire produces Vouvray and Savennières, products of the Chenin Blanc grape (see page 32). Both of these wines are high in acidity, though Vouvray is considerably fruitier, softer, less dry, and more floral than Savennières, which tends to be lemony and minerally. In this region, the Chenin Blanc grape is made into four wine styles: sparkling, dry, off-dry, and sweet. Chenin Blanc has a distinctive honey-floral flavor and great acidity.

A wine called Muscadet made from Melon de Bourgogne grapes (see page 37) rules the mouth of the Loire. Its wine is a crisp white that is dry, slightly musky, and mildly fruity. Drunk young and chilled, it perfectly complements white fish like sole or shellfish. It is widely available and affordable.

ROSÉS FROM THE LOIRE
the Loire Valley is a strong contributor

Rosé wine - the pink wine made when red skins are allowed to ferment for a brief period of time in the grape juice—is made in most winemaking regions around the world. But it is famous in the Loire. Many people feel a bit guilty about enjoying rosé wine, but they shouldn't. Many rosés are quite fabulous, especially those made with Cabernet Franc (see pages 44) and Pinot Noir (see page 46). Rosé wines are white wines with a hint of tannin and make a delightful light beverage that goes beautifully with light meals of fish or chicken.

alsace

*Wines with
a more robust
style*

Alsace has been a sticking point between the French and Germans for centuries. Just look at a map. It lies in the northeast corner of France, just across the Rhine from Germany and set apart from the rest of France by the Vosges Mountains. Little wonder, then, that the style and character of Alsatian wine is more German than French.

The region produces primarily white wines from Riesling, Sylvaner, and Gewürztraminer grapes (see pages 33–35)—varieties commonly used for German wines. However, it also uses Pinot Blanc, Pinot Gris, Pinot Noir, and Muscat varieties to make versatile, food-friendly wines. Grape variety is important in selecting an Alsatian wine, as its wines are named for their variety rather than their region—unlike other French wines.

The climate of Alsace gives its whites fuller body and stronger alcohol content than its German counterparts. These qualities also make them more austere and drier. They are almost always stored in non-oak barrels, so their fruity, spicy character predominates.

Alsatian wines increasingly have status and popularity, as witnessed by the 50 Alsatian vineyards that have been awarded grand cru status. In Alsace's case, the designation applies to wines of particular varieties, and only four have been granted the honor: Riesling, Gewürztraminer, Muscat, and Pinot Gris.

In Alsace, the Pinot Gris wines are known as Tokay Pinot Gris and are full-bodied white wines with peach and banana flavors coupled with nutty, smoky overtones. They are even more powerful than Gewürztraminer, but age beautifully. They also produce an exquisite late-harvest sweet wine.

ASK THE EXPERTS

Why aren't Alsatian wines named by their region?
Because they're named for their varietal grape. Chalk it up to another peculiarity of a region that's changed hands between France and Germany in recent centuries.

Why do gourmets drink so much Gewürztraminer?
Although some people find Gewürztraminer overwhelming, that same strength makes it a perfect partner for such rich, strong-flavored foods as pungent cheeses and foie gras. It goes beautifully with vegetarian dishes, especially those with squash, potato, and sweet potato bases. With its high alcohol content and low acidity, it complements cream soups and spicy ethnic dishes, such as Indian, Thai, Vietnamese, and Chinese.

champagne

The essence of effervescence

Champagne is one of the most famous French wines of all time. Yet weak imitations of French Champagne sneak their way into the market. These sparkling wines are called "champagne" with a small "c" and are sold the world over. Although the United States, Australia, and other countries can brand their sparkling wine as champagne, it can't be considered Champagne with a capital C unless it is made in the Champagne region of France by the so-called **méthode champenoise**, the traditional, time-consuming production process for making Champagne. Méthode champenoise produces the second fermentation that results in carbonation in the bottle. The wine must ferment slowly in the bottle for at least one year, but many producers allow it to stay "on the yeast" for five years or more. (See pages 16–17 for more.)

French regulations also stipulate that a winemaker can only use three grape varieties, in varying blends, to make Champagne: Pinot

Noir (for body), Pinot Meunier (for fruitiness), and Chardonnay (for finesse). Usually the percentage is two thirds black (or red) grapes (Pinot Noir and Pinot Meunier) to one third white grapes (Chardonnay). Champagne is "white" because only grape juices are used, no red-colored skin. Champagnes made entirely from Chardonnay grapes are called blanc de blancs.

ASK THE EXPERTS

I received a marvelous bottle of Dom Perignon as a gift. Should I allow it to age a few years before drinking it?
No need. Champagne is ready to drink as soon as it is put on sale. A year or two of aging will not harm the Champagne, but it is not necessary.

What does brut mean?
"Brut" is French for "dry," which in winetasting means the opposite of sweet. It is used on labels of very dry Champagne. "Extra Dry" on a Champagne bottle sounds like it is the driest, however it is not. Extra Dry champagnes are actually slightly less dry than Brut.

What's the difference between vintage and nonvintage Champagne? Vintage Champagne is made entirely from grapes produced that year without blending them with wines reserved from previous harvests, and is aged longer in the producer's cellar. Vintage Champagne may be more full-bodied and complex than nonvintage. About 85 percent of Champagne, however, is made by blending grapes from various vintages. These are called "NV" (nonvintage). Blending several vintages enables producers to achieve a consistent style.

Am I a philistine because I like pink Champagne?
Absolutely not! Although it has a bad rep, pink Champagne is just rosé wine produced in the méthode champenoise (the juice is strained through the skins of Pinot Noir grapes.) True pink Champagne is one of the most lucious wines in the world.

Perrier-Jouët

sauternes & other sweet wines

The art of making late-harvest wines

France produces sweet wines in almost all of its major wine-producing areas. Its most famous sweet wine is made in a region of Bordeaux called Sauternes.

Just as Bordeaux reds set the standard for the world's red wines, Sauternes serves as the benchmark for sweet wines. Sauternes are made mostly from Sémillon grapes (see page 36), which provide body and fruitiness; some Sauternes also are blended with Sauvignon Blanc grapes (see page 30), which contribute acidity. The marvelous flavor of Sauternes is due to the work of *Botrytis cinerea*, the so-called noble rot, a fungus that attacks late-harvest grapes and gives them their unique flavor. The best Sauternes have a luscious, fruity sweetness that is described as apricot, pineapple, and orange peel with undertones of vanilla, toffee, and honey.

Very near the Sauternes region are the regions of Cadillac, Loupiac, Sainte-Croix-du-Mont, and Cérons, which produce somewhat lighter, simpler wines in the same style as Sauternes. Not only are they delicious, they are less expensive. Of lesser fame but not lesser quality are the late-harvest wines from the Loire Valley (made with the Chenin Blanc grape) and Alsace.

ASK THE EXPERTS

Why should I buy a Sauternes in a half-bottle?
A half bottle (375 ml) serves about four glasses, which is usually enough to drink with dessert. Open another half-bottle if you need more!

Why is Sauternes so expensive?
In addition to the usual reasons that one wine can be pricier than another (see page 73), late-harvest grapes include higher labor costs. Each berry is picked by hand, only selecting the fully mature berries at each picking. Thus, a vineyard often must be harvested repeatedly, from 4 to 10 times per vintage.

What goes well with a French dessert wine?
Sauternes partners beautifully with two celebrated French foods: Roquefort cheese and foie gras, the goose liver specialty of Périgord and Alsace. The sweet, fruity flavors of the wine contrast wonderfully with the pungent flavors of the Roquefort. Sauternes' sweetness is mysteriously enhanced by foie gras. Sauternes also goes beautifully with caviar, truffled pâtés, custard-based desserts like crème brûlée, or if you prefer something a bit simpler, with ripe fruits, berries, and nuts.

answers to common questions

Why do French wines have such a good reputation?

France has been growing grapes and producing wine for a long time—and the country takes its wine consumption very seriously. Just one look at the Appellation d'Origine Controlée regulations, for example, indicates the level of detail in the French classification system. France also benefits from having various climates in its many wine-producing regions—giving it the ability to produce a wide variety of wine.

Are the AOC regulations reliable?

Here's the rule of thumb: the more detail that is provided on the label, the greater the likelihood that you're buying a quality wine. However, one year's bad weather can dampen the winemaking skills of even the best vineyards; and all winemakers, even the best-rated vineyards, sometimes fail to make great wine. On the other hand, what the French designate a mere "table wine" can be utterly delicious.

Why don't French winemakers filter their wine?

Filtering wine means filtering out the particles from the stems and seeds that form sediment in the bottom of a wine bottle. Most French winemakers feel that removing these particles harms the wine's character. Others believe filtering makes a more stable wine. Again, it is a question of taste, but most good French wines are not filtered.

How important is a wine's vintage?

A wine's vintage year is important for two reasons. First, the weather determines the quality of the wines in any region. All winemakers strive to make the very best wines every year; however, nature determines how good the wine can be. There are always exceptionally great years (about twice each decade) and to a lesser extent, exceptionally poor ones.

For red wines, often great vintages yield rich but tannic wines that require longer periods of bottle age, whereas less great, but still good, years are more ready to enjoy upon release. It can be very confusing, but a good vintage chart is the key to understanding it all.

The second reason vintage is important is so that you, the consumer, know how old a wine is when you buy it or consume it. Without vintages, no one would know how old any bottle is.

HELFPUL RESOURCES

MAGAZINES

Decanter
A British-based monthly magazine that covers international wines, but especially classic European wines (French and Italian). For subscription information, call: 800-875-2997

BOOKS

Hugh Johnson's Pocket Encyclopedia of Wine 2000
by Hugh Johnson
The Free Press

The Wine Spectator's Essentials of Wine
by Harvey Steiman
Running Press

7

Italian Wines

about italian wines

Sunny wines from sunny climes

A bottle of wine and a bottle of mineral water are universally present on the Italian table at lunch or dinner. This casual approach to wine is both a strength and weakness for Italian wine's reputation. Many once considered Italy the source of cheap table wine, when in fact it produces some of the world's finest vintage wines.

Wine is made in every part of Italy, from the arid outcroppings of Sicily in the south to the misty foothills of the Alps in the north. Perhaps that is why Italy is the world's largest wine producer. The country is divided into twenty winemaking regions or zones. Each zone is dominated by the variety of grapes that thrive in its particular soil and climate. Some of the Italian grape varieties used in making red wines are Nebbiolo, Barbera, Lambrusco, and Sangiovese. White varieties include Cortese, Trebbiano, Moscato.

Three of Italy's wine regions are such great producers that the names of the wines made there are known around the world: Barolo from the northwestern zone of Piedmont; Chianti from Tuscany, in the north-central region; Soave, Valpolicella, and Bardolino from the northeastern region known as the Veneto.

Today the Italians also grow the traditional French Merlot varietals (see page 000), such as the Cabernet Sauvignon and Chardonnay. To drink one of Italy's wines is to know something of its regions, culture, and history. It's no wonder that Rome gave us Bacchus, the ancient god of wine.

So much was wine a part of ancient Italian history that it was Rome that spread the growing of wine grapes north into Gaul (France) and Germany and west into Spain.

The country is divided into twenty winemaking regions, or zones. Each zone is dominated by the variety of grapes that thrive in its particular soil and climate—for example, the Nebbiolo grape in the Piedmont region, the Sangiovese and Vernaccia grapes in Tuscany, Trebbiano variety in the northeastern zone of the Veneto, Lambrusco grapes from the Emilia-Romagna region around Bologna, Malvasia grapes from the Latium zone around Rome.

ASK THE EXPERTS

Do the Italians have a wine regulatory system like the French?
The Italian wine regulatory system is called the Denominazione di Origine Controllata, or the DOC. Like the French AOC (see page 90), it sets the standards for how wines are made, how much alcohol they can contain, and, among other things, how they should look and taste. Wines that make the cut have the DOC on their label; wines that don't are called **vino da tavola** (or table wine). However, as with the French AOC, the DOC rules (which went into effect in 1966) have loopholes. The result is that some inferior wines can get a DOC label, particularly if they are made the old-fashioned way, while some excellent wines that use new production methods can't.

What is Italian table wine? Is it worth buying?
The designation table wine, or vino da tavola, generally indicates that a wine is of a lower rank than wines that carry a DOC or registered place-name on their labels. A table wine may or may not be labeled with its geographic name or Indicazione Geografica Tipica (IGT). With or without the IGT designation, a vino da tavola is always an acceptable choice for everyday use or large-scale, casual entertaining.

barolo

A robust red

The mountainous region of northwestern Italy is known as the Piedmont. It is home to a luscious grape called Nebbiolo which is named for the fog that aids in its ripening. From these grapes comes a robust red wine called Barolo.

High in tannin, acidity, and alcohol, a young Barolo is a jolt to the taste buds. That's why all Barolos are aged at least two years in wooden casks. Some vintages, marked *riserva* and *riserva speciale* are allowed to mature over five years. This process tames its intensity and develops its complexity, or layers of flavor. A slow sip of a well-aged Barolo can bring with it the musky scent of truffles (mushrooms)—another Italian natural treasure. A mature Barolo at its best is often compared to well-aged French Burgundy. A fine Barolo can cost between $35 and $195. The harvests of 1996 and 1997 were excellent in Piedmont, making those years prime vintage years (see page 170). While still a bit young, Barolos from those years are a premium wine choice, ideal for future special occasions.

A NOTE ABOUT TANNINS

Barolos have a particularly high percentage of tannin—the substance found in the skin, seeds, and stems of grapes that is more prevalent in red wine than white because the juice is "steeped" in the skins. Tannins (see page 12) have been regarded with suspicion as the cause of a blotchy skin reaction known as the wine blush. Tannin can be beneficial. Some recent reserach shows that it contains antioxidants that help prevent arterial clogging and lower the risk of cardiovascular disease.

WINE AND FOOD

A glass of red wine goes well with a wedge of hard, aged Italian cheese. Try Reggiano, the prince of Parmesans, or an aged Pecorino with a glass of Barolo and you'll understand why many people feel that the best things in life are Italian. If you've never tried fresh Parmesan cheese on its own, you are in for a treat. And if you think you know red wine, you'll be stunned by your first sip of Barolo.

chianti

*From
ordinary
to classic*

To most foreigners, Chianti *is* Italian wine. For decades, straw-cased bottles of Chianti on red-checked tablecloths were essential to the atmosphere of Italian-American restaurants. The light, dry, yet fruity quality of the wine with its slight scent of cherries made Chianti a favorite choice to accompany Italian dishes. Then slowly, over the years, the quality of Chianti took a turn for the worse. Why, you ask? Read on.

Chianti is produced from red Sangiovese and Canaiolo grapes grown in Tuscany, one of Italy's most beautiful regions. Until recently, this ancient wine was produced from blending the red Sangiovese and Canaiolo grapes with 5 percent white Malvasia or

Trebbiano grapes to cut harshness and make the wine drinkable at a younger age. But perhaps to satisfy demand or save on costs, the percentage of these white grapes steadily increased to between 10 and 30 percent, resulting in a thinner, more ordinary wine.

By the mid-1980s, the best producers were so unhappy with the quality of Chianti and Chianti Classico that the percentage of white to red grapes was reduced to the original 5 percent. Italy's wine regulatory commission then awarded Chianti a special label—DOCG (Denominazione di Origine Controllata e Garantita)—a classification given to only the finest wines. Classico had become truly classic.

Millions of bottles of Chianti are produced each year in Tuscany, but only about a third of them are Classico, which comes from the traditional heart of the Chianti zone between Florence and Siena. Of these elite Chiantis, the specially aged riserva is the most prized. Some of the great Chianti producers of Tuscany are Castello d'Albola, Melini, Nozzole, Villa Banfi, Frescobaldi, Antinori, and Ruffino. Chianti remains one of Italy's most reasonably priced wines, from the ordinary Chianti, which sells for as little as $6, to Chianti Classico, which ranges from $10 to $36.

Chianti Rufina
Remole

PETER SELECTS

- **Chianti Rufina Remole Marchese di Frescobaldi**
  $8–$10

- **Chianti Classico Castello de Volpaia**
  $15–$20

- **Chianti Classico Riserva Villa Antinori**
  $17–$20

- **Chianti Classico Riserva Ducale Ruffino**
  $20–$24

vernaccia di san gimignano

A Tuscan white goddess

Italy is often considered a red wine nation, but this is to neglect some of its delightful whites, which are becoming popular in and outside the country. One of the most delicious whites is produced halfway between Florence and Siena in Tuscany by wineries near the ancient walled village of San Gimignano. The stone towers of this 13th-century town look down on a peaceful tapestry of olive trees and vineyards where growers tend golden Vernaccia grapes.

The wine is almost as old as the village. In its medieval version, Vernaccia was a powerful barrel-aged wine. Today's Vernaccia is paler in color and easier on the palate. The original darker version of this wine is still available locally for those who prefer its strong character, but the new Vernaccia is a light, fresh wine that is best when young. It is excellent drunk before meals or with food. Simplicity is its virtue. It combines well with simple chicken, fish, or vegetarian dishes such as frittata. Americans who yearn for Italy but are unable to book an immediate trip can evoke the atmosphere of the suave Tuscan countryside with a glass of Vernaccia di San Gimignano and a slice of good Italian bread drizzled with extra virgin olive oil and a sprinkle of salt.

Most Vernaccias are $12 or less, making them an excellent choice for entertaining. Try the ones produced by Teruzzi & Puthod, San Quirico, Falchini, and Montenidoli.

HOLY WINE!
The spirit of this wine is heavenly

Many Tuscan wineries produce Vin Santo, a topaz-colored dessert wine of ancient origin whose name means "wine of the saints." To make it, white Malvasia grapes are dried, fermented, and sealed in barrels, then subjected to the cold of winter and the heat of summer. The resulting wine may be either dry or sweet and carries a rich, heady aroma. A wine fit for the god Bacchus, Vin Santo may originally have been used for religious purposes. Whatever its origin, it is not for guzzling but for sipping thoughtfully after dinner with an almond-flecked biscotti.

valpolicella

A popular red from Italy's Veneto

The Veneto, a northeastern region of Italy, is marked by contrasts from the rich farmland of the Po delta to the foothills north of Venice, with their views of the Dolomites and Austria beyond. The Veneto is a region of geographic difference that is matched by the variety of its grapes, most of which are grown in the north between Conegliano and Lake Garda.

The wine center of this region is Verona, the ancient city of Romeo and Juliet. Every spring, Verona hosts Italy's biggest wine fair, called Vinitaly. The Veronese red wine best known to wine-lovers outside Italy is Valpolicella, a wine blended from Corvina, Molinara, and Rondinella grapes. Valpolicella is a light, fruity red reminiscent of Chianti but with a hint of almond. Those that have *superiore* on their label have been aged for at least one year. The top of the line Valpolicellas have *classico* on their labels. Valpolicellas are great with Italian food, naturally, but go well with hearty beef and poultry dishes.

ⒶSK THE EXPERTS

Is it okay to chill Italian red wines?

Until recently, Americans tended to serve their reds wines too warm and their whites too cold. Now the trend has swung to cooling reds and warming whites. Some reds, like Bardolino and Chianti, can be cooled to nice effect. Just remember, chilling a wine too much can dull the range of its flavor.

Who are the major producers of Valpolicella?

Bertani and Bolla are two big makers of Valpolicella. Look also for wines made by Allegrini, Lamberti, Alighieri, Tommasi, and Masi. Valpolicellas are a bargain, selling at between $6 and $10.

AMARONE: THE MARRIAGE SAVER
Reconciling never tasted so good

A variety of Valpolicella known as Amarone is a rich red with a great deal of body—and a considerably higher price tag. It gets its unique power from the way its grapes are treated. To make Amarone, ripe grapes are dried for several months on mats before the fermentation process begins. The resulting wine is dry with a rich palate. This red is higher in alcohol content (between 14 and 16 percent) than other Valpolicellas and has gained a reputation for its powerful effect. Marriage counselors around Verona advise troubled couples to "try the Amarone cure" before seeing a lawyer.

bardolino

*Another great
red from Veneto*

From the same part of Northern Italy as Valpolicella comes the less well-known Bardolino, a lighter-bodied red than Valpolicella but with similar freshness and acidity. Bardolino shows the variety that the Veneto's winemakers can achieve by combining the trio of grapes—Corvina Veronese, Rondinella, and Molinara—that go into making so many of the region's reds.

This is a young wine with a lower alcohol content (minimum 10.5 percent) compared to Valpolicella Amarone (14 to 16 percent). As a result, Bardolino tastes best when slightly chilled. It's a delicious summer wine that makes an easygoing accompaniment to outdoor grilling. Bardolinos are reasonably priced, within the $10 range.

PINOT GRIGIO
A popular white grape the world over

Americans are finding the white Italian wine, Pinot Grigio, a nice change from Chardonnay. In most wine stores and on most restaurant menus in America, a selection of Italian Pinot Grigios (usually priced under $10, but occasionally in the $12 to $15 range) is available.

Pinot Grigio is a varietal grape that grows throughout the world. In France and the U.S.A. it is known as Pinot Gris (see page 36). When grown in northeastern Italy it makes a pleasant, dry-ish white wine that, because of the easy cultivation of the Pinot Grigio grapes, can be marketed and sold relatively cheaply and profitably. The fact is, most Pinot Grigio varietal wines are refreshing—great everyday wines—but very often lack distinction.

ASK THE EXPERTS

If a wine from Italy doesn't have DOC on the label, what do I look for?

Italian wine labels are complicated, and there are no set rules to interpreting them. The label may contain some or all of the following: the name of the region where the wine is produced, the name of the town near the vineyard, the name of the grapes, the name of the wine producer, and of course, the year of production. Italian wines are usually known by the name of the town where the grapes are grown, such as Barolo, or the region, such as Chianti. When in doubt, a DOC label guarantees a wine that meets government standards but may range in taste from ordinary to superb. No wine should be ignored merely because it lacks the DOC label.

soave

*Italy's most
famous white*

Superior Italian reds outnumber whites in Italy, but a range of charming whites is available. Soave is probably the most famous. This white wine has a light, uncomplicated taste that is popular with Americans. Named for the village of Soave in the Veneto region, it is a blend of white Garganega and Trebbiano di Soave grapes. The Garganega grape is grown only in this northeastern region and gives the wine its dry yet fruity palate. A fine Soave Classico is made from grapes grown in the central part of the zone.

Soave deserves its reputation as a great partygoer. It should be drunk chilled and as young as possible. It makes a fine choice to sip by itself or to accompany summer fare at the buffet table. Try a Soave Classico with fish or risotto.

Like Valpolicella and Bardolino, Soave is reasonably priced at about $10. Bolla is the Soave producer best known in the U.S. Bolla was established in the 19th century and is now run by the Bolla brothers, who operate a big, sleek production facility near Verona. Other venerable producers of Soave are Bertani, Masi, and Guerrieri Rizzardi. Pieropan makes a prizewinning Soave Classico.

FIRST PERSON DISASTER

Overchill

One day last May, my boss invited me to a dinner to celebrate the end of tax season. On the way home from work I splurged on a terrific Soave Classico. The day was warm and my refrigerator was elderly. Would there be time to properly chill the wine? I came up with the bright idea to turn up my freezer to high and quick-chill the wine. One hour later, as I was about to leave, I opened the freezer. The bottle of wine looked like a high school chemistry experiment gone wrong. The wine, obeying the laws of nature, had expanded as it froze and pushed the cork out of the bottle. My freezer was now coated with frozen Soave. Needless to say, I left the bottle thawing in the sink. I told my boss about the wine and he laughed. He said you can keep a bottle of wine in the freezer for only 15 minutes or else you earn the wrath of Mother Nature. In wine as in taxes, there are apparently no safe short cuts.

—Valerie M., Atlanta, Georgia

answers to common questions

Should I order only Italian wines at an Italian restaurant?

Most authentic Italian restaurants will have a good wine list made up predominantly of Italian wines. If you're not sure what to order, ask your waiter, especially if he or she is from Italy, where knowledge of wine and food seems practically bred in the bone. They should be able to help you select a wine for your palate and budget.

Why is a fiasco not a bad thing for a Chianti?

The traditional straw casing of the Chianti bottle is known as fiasco. How the word fiasco came to mean what it does today—a failure or flop—nobody knows. There may be a link with Italy's long history of comic theatre and opera. But one thing is certain: fiasco is no fiasco when it is cradling a bottle of Chianti.

What's a super-Tuscan?

In the 1970s, a number of Tuscan producers began creating new wines (Solaia and Tignanello are two famous examples) that became known among wine lovers as super-Tuscans. These wines were red blends (usually Sangiovese and Cabernet Sauvignon). Today, producers also use other grapes, including Merlot and Syrah, among others. Although they bear the vino da tavola (table wine) designation on their labels, super-Tuscans are expensive, but without exception they are just that—exceptional.

What is grappa and how does it relate to wine?

An Italian brandy that is becoming popular in the U.S. is grappa, an afterdinner drink. The old-fashioned grappas were made from leftover grape skins, stems, and twigs, which were then combined with water and sugar and fermented to produce a powerful, clear brandy with a high alcohol content. Originally considered a peasant drink to be downed by the shot (a couple of ounces drunk straight in one gulp), a new kind of highly perfumed and delicious grappa made by specialty distillers from the first pressings of the grapes is now showing up on trendy restaurant tables accompanied by a cup of espresso.

Does Italian wine culture go back to Roman times?

It would seem so. The ancient Romans knew how to party—and like the ancient Greeks, they made wine a central part of their gatherings. Romans didn't engage in casual drinking (except for a quick shot of wine that was sometimes consumed at breakfast). They reserved drinking for gatherings at their main meal in the evening. At a formal dinner, the first course, similar to the modern Italian antipasto, consisted of fish or vegetables. Roasted meat and fowl came in the next course, then bread, fruit, and sweet jams. After dinner was cleared away, the drinking began. The host led his guests in a toast or ritual libation that dated back to the ancient Greek tradition of toasting the wine god Dionysus (Bacchus to Romans).

What are "boutique" vini da tavola?

These are wines, mostly from Tuscany, that are made from French grapes, such as Cabernet Sauvignon and Merlot. Some experts consider these "boutique" wines to be among Italy's finest "new wave" wines.

HELFPUL RESOURCES

BOOKS

The Italian Wine Guide: Where to Go and What to See, Drink, and Eat

from *The Touring Club of Italy*

A good guide for travelers—armchair or real—who wish to know all about Italian vineyards and their wines.

8

American Wines

wine in america

*New World
wine*

Arriving in the New World in the 1600s, settlers discovered native grape varieties, now known as *labrusca* grapes, growing wild. Alas, these don't produce as fine a wine as the European *vinifera* varieties (such as Cabernet Sauvignon, Chardonnay, and Cabernet Franc). Later, wine fanciers like Thomas Jefferson imported and planted vinifera rootstocks from France. But the Old World grapes failed to thrive, making Jefferson a very frustrated vintner. In the 19th century, European immigrants arrived in California with vines from the old country. Given the similarities in climate to France and Italy, these grapes flourished.

The next step was the creation of new wineries and new winemaking styles. Unfortunately, as wine production and the wine industry grew, Prohibition arrived, lasting from 1920 to 1933. American wine did not fully recover from the effects of Prohibition until the

1960s and 1970s, when people started becoming more adventuresome with their food and drink.

Then in 1976 came the crowning moment. A California 1973 vintage Chateau Montelena Chardonnay won a blind winetasting contest in Paris. French expert winetasters were stunned to learn that they'd chosen a California Chardonnay over their own premier white Burgundies. American wine had finally come into its own.

THE DEADLY PHYLLOXERA
It nearly ended it all

The grapes of eastern United States may have been of poor quality, but they were hardy and abundant. Perhaps they could improve the yield of the more delicate European grapes, or so thought some winemakers in 1860. They took some cuttings back to Europe and grafted them onto European rootstock.

No one knew that the East Coast grapes harbored an insidious problem: they were home to a deadly aphidlike insect called phylloxera. This tiny insect attacks the rootstock and starves the vine, resulting in poor fruit yields. Within a few years, phylloxera had spread throughout numerous European vineyards and decimated the more delicate European vine stock. The solution was to find a rootstock that was resistant to phylloxera. In America, one particular rootstock—the **vitis riparia**—was resistant to the aphid. This grape rootstock was grafted onto the weakened European vine stock and the problem was solved. Does every fine wine from France have a bit of America in it? Depends on whom you ask.

In the 1890s phylloxera struck in California, where it attacked those grapes that were originally vitis vinifera planted by European settlers. The vigorous vitis riparia was used to cure the problem. But the insect returned once more to California in the 1980s. This time winemakers turned to science and created new strains of vine root stocks that were resistant to the deadly phylloxera.

napa valley

America's Bordeaux

French wines owe much to France's mild but varied climate: cool northern regions for white grapes, warm southern slopes for its full-bodied red grapes. The same happy climate conditions can be found in California, starting with Napa Valley—California's own Bordeaux (see page 92). All the major grapes are grown in Napa. Cabernet Sauvignon and Merlot lead the pack as the wines most Americans associate with Napa, followed by Chardonnay, Zinfandel, and the increasingly popular Pinot Noir.

Napa-grown Cabernet Sauvignon grapes produce fruit-filled, full-bodied red wines that are award winners. Chardonnay grapes, when fermented and aged in oak, produce Napa's most complex and prized white varietal wine. Zinfandel, a grape that grows especially well in California, makes a spicy red wine in all qualities. Merlot yields a velvety smooth wine soft in tannin. Merlot's popularity may be due to its smooth, mellow palate sensation, which contrasts with Napa's more intense and spicy Cabernet.

There are over 200 wineries in the 35-mile stretch of the Napa Valley. The competition and selection is overwhelming and every quality of wine is available, from $5 jug wine to $50 estate-bottled reserves. Most wineries offer tours and winetasting all year round. April and October (for the autumn harvest) are particularly appealing times to soak up this little piece of Eden.

ASK THE EXPERTS

Why is Napa Valley the most famous California wine-growing region?

Because it includes some of the finest wineries in the state, such as Robert Mondavi, Beringer, Heitz Wine Cellars, Joseph Phelps, Franciscan, and Sterling, to name a few. It takes decades to build a winery's reputation and Napa, thanks to its longevity, has the jump on newer regions, such as California's Central Coast.

Why does Napa Valley produce so many different varieties of wine?

The cool ocean air coming north from the San Francisco Bay mixes with the warm inland air to give various regions within Napa Valley unique climates. These regions are called **micro-climates** in the wine world. They are important because subtle changes in temperature can allow for the success of different varieties of grapes. This is why Chardonnay grapes do well in the cooler southern Napa Valley and Cabernet in the warmer north.

*The Hess Collection
Napa Valley Chardonnay*

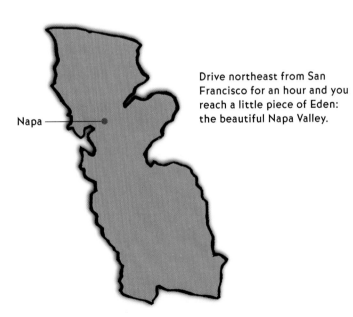

Drive northeast from San Francisco for an hour and you reach a little piece of Eden: the beautiful Napa Valley.

Napa

PETER SELECTS

- **Beaulieu Vineyards "Rutherford" Cabernet Sauvignon**
  Napa Valley $18-$20

- **Joseph Phelps Cabernet Sauvignon**
  Napa Valley $30-$40

- **Caymus Vineyards Cabernet Sauvignon**
  Napa Valley $75-$80

- **Chardonnay Hess Collection Chardonnay**
  Napa Valley $20-$22

- **Shafer Red Shoulder Ranch Chardonnay,**
  Carneros District-
  Napa Valley $38-$42

- **Franciscan Vineyards**
  Oakville Estate
  Napa Valley $17-$20

- **Franciscan Vineyards Cuvée Sauvage**
  Napa Valley $30-$35

sonoma

*Home to
California's oldest
wineries*

Between Napa Valley and the Pacific Ocean lies Sonoma. It is
a cooler region than Napa because ocean breezes and fog seep
through the mountain gaps, making it a haven for numerous grape
varieties. More than 100 wineries grow the complete range of
California's red and white grapes: Chardonnay, Sauvignon Blanc,
Cabernet Sauvignon, Pinot Noir, Merlot, and Zinfandel.

Among Sonoma's wineries are many of California's most prestigious, including Chateau St. Jean, Clos du Bois, Ferrari-Carano,
Iron Horse, Sebastiani Vineyards, and the Simi Winery. It's also
home to F. Korbel, founded in 1882 and still one of California's
major producers of sparkling wine.

Sonoma produces some of the most delicious Zinfandels—a unique
grape variety that grows well in California. It can have a broad range
of incredible flavors, from fruit-intensive with a touch of sweetness,

almost like port, to deep and elegant with blackberry richness—giving a good Cabernet a run for its money. Or it can be lighter, almost like a good Beaujolais—suggesting even a bit of a chill. Among wineries producing the classiest Sonoma Zins are Dry Creek Ridge, St. Francis, and Selby.

Sonoma is also home to the fine wine division of one of the biggest wineries in the world—Gallo. Two brothers, Ernest and Julio, started it in California's Central Valley in Modesto right on the heels of Prohibition in 1933. Through shrewd marketing and smart pricing, they did much to bring wine into American homes. Their moderately priced jug wines, Hearty Burgundy and Chablis Blanc, became the standards for a time. Gallo has evolved with the times and now creates some truly fine Zinfandels and other high-end vintage varietal wines from their Frei, Barelli, and Stefani Ranch vineyards in Sonoma and Northern Sonoma Estates.

GRAPES GET A HIGHER EDUCATION
The art and science of winemaking

In typical American fashion, California winemaking caught up to Europe's with hard work and technology. California winemakers knew they couldn't duplicate ancient European vineyards, so they made the most of what they had: a consistently fine, dry climate for producing ripe fruit and the technology to control and monitor irrigation, soil quality, and rootstock (the lower part of the root, used for plant propagation). The Department of Viticulture and Enology at the University of California at Davis turned the art of winemaking into a high-tech science. Their efforts have enabled winemakers to combat deadly diseases such as the phylloxera, as well as to improve winemaking techniques. The results are wines that now compete successfully with those from Europe.

california's central coast

A cluster of fascinating microclimates

One of the largest vine-growing areas in California also shares the most diverse climate, from cool, fog-drenched Santa Cruz to the golden warmth of the Saint Ynez Valley near Santa Barbara. Ocean humidity and inland heat provide a range of grape-growing microclimates.

The Central Coast, the area between Santa Cruz and Santa Barbara, is an area that produces a wide range of wines. The Pinot Noir grape does well in the coolness of the Santa Cruz Mountains, although Cabernet is still plentiful, and reliable Chardonnay remains the white grape of choice. Just south along the Central Coast, Monterey County devotes over 30,000 acres to all the major varieties of grapes, with Cabernet again taking top prize. Its vineyards stretch from the coastal highlands inland to the Salinas Valley. Of the dozen-plus vineyards in the region, many supply grapes to other wineries as well as making their own wine.

The Santa Maria Valley, San Luis Obispo, and Santa Ynez Valley north of Santa Barbara are the centers of grape production on the South Central Coast. Famous for its rocky outcroppings where sea lions raise their young, San Luis Obispo is now noted for Zinfandel and Cabernet Sauvignon from the Paso Robles region, and Chardonnay from the cool Edna Valley and Arroyo Grande regions. The valleys north of beautiful Santa Barbara produce fine Pinot Noir and Chardonnay grapes.

ASK THE EXPERTS

Does the U.S. have a system to classify wines?
Yes. It's called the American Viticultural Area, or AVA. It defines the various growing regions within the U.S., much like France's AOC (see page 90). For instance, in California the Napa is considered an AVA growing area, as are Sonoma and the Russian River Valley. Oregon and Washington State have several AVAs, as does New York. For a wine to put the AVA on its label, at least 85 percent of the grapes must come from that AVA region.

american sparkling wines

Creating bubbles the modern way

Nothing adds to a celebration like a glass of bubbly, be it a sparkling wine or champagne. For much of the early part of the century, American winemakers made inexpensive sparkling wines, like the sweet, pink, fizzy cold duck, by injecting carbon dioxide into pink wine. But as American tastes evolved, so did techniques for making sparkling wines, with the result that today many fine western state sparkling wines are available from California, Oregon, Washington, and even New Mexico!

Under French law, only sparkling wine that is made in the region of France called Champagne can use the name Champagne (see page 104), but there are many excellent American sparkling wines. One technique big American wineries have been using for decades to make sparkling wines is called the **vat process**. Here wine is put into pressurized tanks so the carbon dioxide created during fermenting is retained. In the U.S., both vat fermentation and the longer classic French method of making the secondary fermentation occur inside sealed bottles are used to produce these wines, with the result that a bottle of home-grown American bubbly can cost anywhere from $8 to $40 depending on the method used to create the bubbles.

The best grapes to use for sparkling wines are underripe, highly acidic grapes grown in cool regions. In the U.S., California and New York State have the longest sparkling wine traditions. Over the past thirty years, a number of famous European sparkling wine and Champagne companies have entered the California market

ASK THE EXPERTS

What does brut mean on a bottle of sparkling wine?
Because very acidic grapes are used to make sparkling wines, winemakers add a little sugar and wine mixture (called a dosage) to the wine to make it a little sweeter. **Brut** means dry in French—dry being the opposite of sweet. **Extra dry** sparklers are ones that have more dosage added and, ironically, are slightly sweeter than Brut.

What is a blanc de blancs sparkling wine?
Most sparkling wines are made from blends of various grapes. Some winemakers are now making sparkling wines from specific varietals, such as Chardonnay or Pinot Noir. A blanc de blancs is made entirely from Chardonnay grapes.

oregon & washington state

Where Pinot Noir and Merlot thrive

Oregon is the home of a young but thriving wine industry that centers on the Pinot Noir, a red grape variety that does very well in Oregon's cool climate. Oregon's prime grape-growing region is located in the Willamette Valley, south of Portland. This region benefits from coastal air currents that red grapes demand. Oregon also grows Chardonnay grapes, but the white grape that puts Oregon on the map is Pinot Gris, a grape renowned in northern Italy as Pinot Grigio. Pinot Gris is lighter and younger than Chardonnay, with a less overbearing palate.

Washington State

Led by the Chateau Ste. Michelle Winery, Washington State, Oregon's northern neighbor, has built up a formidable wine industry. While Oregon's grapes are grown close to the coast, Washington's vineyards are primarily located in the hotter, dryer valleys to the east of the Cascade Mountains.

Washington's arid but beautiful Yakima and Columbia valleys grow all the major red and white varieties. The state, however, is best known for its red grapes, principally Merlot. Over the last decade, Americans have discovered the appeal of this Washington State–grown red varietal wine with its velvety palate appeal.

PETER SELECTS

OREGON

● **Willamette Valley Vineyards "Whole Cluster" Pinot Noir** $15–$25

● **Domaine Drouhin Pinot Noir** $33–$40

● **Adelsheim Vineyards Pinot Noir** $25–$40

WASHINGTON STATE

● **Chateau Ste. Michelle Winery** Produces very good quality Chardonnay, Sauvignon Blanc, Merlot, Cabernet Sauvignon, and sparkling wines. Ste. Michelle also owns the Columbia Crest brand.

● **Hedges Merlot/Cabernet** Columbia Valley, Washington $11–$13

● **Hedges Three Vineyards Cabernet Sauvignon** Columbia Valley, Washington $27–$30

● **Woodward Canyon Chardonnay** Columbia Valley, Washington, $30–$35

ABOUT ORGANIC WINE
Growing natural and chemical-free

The health-food trends of the 1970s have trickled down to wine. Concern over pesticide residues in grapes has led some growers to grow grapes organically.

In organic viticulture, mechanical weeding replaces herbicides, beneficial insects are used instead of pesticides, and natural mulches and fertilizers substitute for chemical ones. Often, in the winemaking process, additives such as sulfites, used as a preservative, are avoided.

Organic wineries are beginning to pro-duce some good wines. Bonterra Vineyards in Mendocino, California, makes organic wine in all the major red and white varietals and blends. Fitzpatrick Winery near Placerville, California, in the Sierra foothills, produces all the major California wine varieties from organically grown grapes. China Blend Vineyards in Kettle Falls, Washington, makes unsulfited organic reds and whites. Organic wines tend to be priced in the medium ($9 to $14) to expensive ($20 and more) range.

new york state

Home to America's oldest winery

New York established its successful wine industry in the Hudson Valley and Finger Lakes regions first by hybridizing classic European **vinifera** (grape varieties such as Cabernet Sauvignon) with more winter-tolerant vines. Today Chardonnay, Pinot Noir, Riesling, Sauvignon Blanc, Merlot, and Cabernet Sauvignon are among the varieties grown, as well as the native American labrusca varieties, such as Catawba, Delaware, and Niagara grapes.

New York's vineyards were originally clustered around the Finger Lakes, south of Lake Ontario, along the Hudson River, and also in western New York State on the shores of Lake Erie. (The Brotherhood Winery, west of the Hudson River in Orange County, is the oldest winery in the United States.) Over the last three decades, big business has bought and expanded older wineries such as Gold Seal, Taylor, and Great Western, while at the same time dozens of small new boutique wineries have opened, particularly on Long Island's North and South forks.

OTHER AMERICAN WINE REGIONS
Growing grapes everywhere

Every state except Alaska and North Dakota cultivates grapes and makes wine—even Hawaii. Alaska is outside the viticultural temperature zone, but—who knows—maybe someone will manage to grow some sort of useful grape there. It's not impossible, given technical advances. Aside from the best-known winegrowing regions in the U.S., in recent years Arizona, New Mexico, Texas, Virginia, North Carolina, Ohio, and Pennsylvania have turned out some interesting wines.

North fork

The Hamptons

PETER SELECTS

NEW YORK STATE
- **Schneider Vineyards Cabernet Franc**
  North Fork, Long Island
  $22-$25

- **Wolffer Vineyards Merlot**
  The Hamptons, Long Island $19-$21

- **Paumanok Chardonnay**
  North Fork, Long Island
  $17-$20

- **Potato Barn White**
  North Fork, Long Island
  $13-$15

- **Wolffer Estate Selection Chardonnay**

The Hamptons $25-$30
- **Millbrook Vineyards Chardonnay**
  Hudson Valley, New York
  $13-$16

- **Millbrook Vineyards Reserve Chardonnay**
  Hudson Valley, New York
  $18-$20

- **Millbrook Vineyards Tocai Friulano**
  Hudson Valley, New York
  $13-$15

OTHER STATES
VIRGINIA
- **Oakencroft Vineyards Chardonnay**

Charlottesville, Virginia
$15-$17
- **Horton Viognier**
  Virginia $22-$25

PENNSYLVANIA
- **Chaddsford Winery Philip Roth Vineyard Chardonnay**
  Chadds Ford, PA, $25-$30

ARIZONA
- **Callaghan Vineyards Cabernet Sauvignon**
  $20-$30

NEW MEXICO
- **Gruet Brut Sparkling Wine**
  $15-$17

answers to common questions

Why are American wines named for grape variety rather than location?
Prior to Prohibition, in the U.S. location was less important to winemakers than the variety of grapes grown. Hence, American wines tended to be called by the name of their grape variety (Chardonnay, Zinfandel, and Cabernet being the most popular), rather than their region. In the past five decades, the industry has more and more come to recognize the importance of climate and soil as a guide to which grapes do best where.

Why are America's native labrusca grapes considered inferior to European vinifera grapes?
Virtually all wine experts agree that native American grapes don't make good wine. It all comes down to quality of taste. About the best you can say for Concord and other native labrusca grapes of the northeast is that they make pretty good table juice and jelly (think Welch's). Today, a few New York and midwestern vineyards still produce wine exclusively from labrusca varieties that thrive in their native environment. Some have even produced successful crossbreeds with European vinifera vines. These wineries are adapting their products to changing taste and producing | labrusca-based wines that are less sweet—and gaining attention for their efforts.

Can you visit American wineries?
Almost always, yes. Americans are fantastic marketers, and one of the best ways to sell wine is to let people tour the winery and taste the wine. Most wineries are willing to do this free because people will usually buy several bottles or a case on the spot. However, wine cannot always be shipped across state lines by wineries (see page 87). Check the regulations in your home state before asking that wine be shipped there.

HELFPUL RESOURCES

MAGAZINES
California Grapevine
Features the results of ongoing comparative tastings of recent winery releases by varietal wine type with comprehensive tasting notes, group and individual rankings within each tasting. Wines begin at about $12. Published six times a year. Annual subscription $35. For subscription information, call: 858-457-4818, or fax: 858-457-3676

BOOKS
Wine Spectator's California Wine
By James Laube
Running Press
The author draws on over 50,000 wine tastings to present a cogent refernce work on California's many wines.

NEWSLETTER
Connoisseur's Guide to California Wine
A valuable monthly newsletter that gives recommendations and comprehensive in-depth tasting notes on California varietal wines. Wines begin at about $10. Annual subscription: $50. For subscription information, call: 510-865-3150

WEB SITE
Wineexplorer.com
Explores the wine country lifestyle and is an excellent guide for visits to wineries.

9

Other Old & New World Wines

old & new world wines

Many are exceptional

Two thousand years ago in the Old World, Rome's military legions planted grapevines in every region they conquered. After all, they had to have something to drink wherever they ruled and in those days wine did not travel well. When the Roman Empire collapsed, Catholic friars and monks in Europe took over tending the abandoned vines and continued refining the winemaking process.

When European explorers set sail in the 17th and 18th centuries, they carried European wines as well as European vines. As the

Romans had done in the Old World, these adventurers founded vineyards in the New World to ensure a ready supply of their favorite beverage.

Although the wine regions of the New World are diverse and far-flung, they all aspire to the great tradition of winemaking that was perfected over the centuries in Europe. In the 20th century, technological innovations developed in American laboratories have greatly enhanced viticulture and improved the quality winemaking worldwide.

For new consumers of wine as well as for dedicated connoisseurs, this means better-quality wines from all over the world at more affordable prices. It is a harvest of delight.

ASK THE EXPERTS

Are other European wines harder to find than French and Italian?
Your selection will not be as great when you hunt down wines from these other countries, but most good wine shops should have some selections for you to try. If you can't find something, ask the shop staff if they'll take a special order.

Do all European wines come under European Union or EU regulations?
No, only those wines grown in EU member countries must comply with EU regulations. Switzerland and Bulgaria, for instance, are two wine-producing countries that are currently not in the European Union.

Do other countries have their own regulations?
Yes. Like France, most countries have found that government regulations help to ensure the quality of their wine.

spanish wines

A prolific producer where Sherry still reigns

When most people think of Spanish wine, they think of Sherry. But in fact, Spain is the third largest wine-producing country in the world, after France and Italy. Spain is known for its red wines, made principally from the Tempranillo grape—the country's greatest red variety.

Spain's most famous wine-producing area has long been Rioja in north central Spain, from which some stunning red wines hail. Moreover, today many other wine regions, such as Ribera del Duero, are creating excellent wines.

One of Spain's most delightful contributions to the wine world is its sparkling wine, known as Cava. Like Champagne, Cava is made by fermenting the wine in the bottle. Cava uses local Spanish grapes that give it an earthier flavor than French Champagne. Freixenet and Codorníu are the two major Spanish wineries that produce Cava.

SHERRY

For sublime sipping and cooking

Spain's great gift to the world of wine is Sherry, a premier fortified wine. Named for Jerez—pronounced "haireth"—de la Frontera (an old Moorish town in southern Spain), Sherry is made primarily from Palomino grapes (a variety that fails when used to make any other sort of wine).

Sherry has an undeserved reputation as a sickly sweet wine for Victorian grannies. Although there are sweet Sherries, most Sherry is dry. In fact, the two most basic types of Sherry are dry: fino (light, very dry) and oloroso (richer, but also dry). From these two basic types come the famous nutlike amontillado and the generously scented and richly flavored palo cortado. Dry Sherry is best served at room temperature and makes a lovely pre- or afterdinner drink. The sweet Sherries, such as cream Sherry and Moscatel, are created by adding sweet must—the juice of freshly crushed grapes that includes pulp, skin, and seeds—to the blend. Fino Sherries are best drunk slightly chilled and served as a pre-dinner drink. A note to cooks: use a good quality dry Sherry, not a sweet one, when cooking. There is nothing like dry Sherry to bring out the flavor of a stew or hearty soup.

FIRST PERSON DISASTER

Sorry substitutes

I was visiting friends and wanted to help out with dinner. I offered to make a roast I often make at home. I knew the recipe by heart. It called for 1 cup of soy sauce, 1 cup dry Sherry, and 1/2 cup honey and various spices. My hosts didn't have any Sherry. After rummaging around their cupboards, I found some red cooking wine and used that instead. Not a good idea. The roast tasted pretty awful, as if it had been sitting in salty vinegar. I went in and tasted the so-called cooking wine and it was awful. I should have substituted a half cup of good red wine and a half cup of brandy. A friend later told me that "cooking wine" was a term coined in the 19th century when ladies of the house salted the wine so the cooks wouldn't imbibe too much when cooking with it.

— Elizabeth K., Selma, Alabama

portuguese wines

A treasure trove of fortified wines

Port, a favorite afterdinner drink, rules Portugal's wine reputation as much as Sherry dominates Spain's. About the only Portuguese wine that most Americans will remember is Mateus or Lancer's—two Portuguese rosé wines that used to be very popular among newly initiated wine drinkers. These days, however, Portugal produces many notable wines, among them a white wine called Vinho Verde and a red wine called Barca Velha.

Portugal is also home to Madeira, which along with Port and Sherry is one of the world's great fortified wines (wine to which alcohol has been added). Madeira is made from grapes grown on the island province of Madeira. It is produced in a unique way by being "baked" in a special process after fermentation. Almost all Madeira is made from white grapes but with aging becomes deep amber in color. The style will be listed as dry (Rainwater), medium-dry (Sercial), medium-sweet (Boal or Bual), or sweet (Malmsey).

PORT
A favorite afterdinner drink

Port (or Porto as the Portuguese call it) is a sweet fortified wine. Imitations abound, so for true Portuguese Port, look for the word "Porto" on the label. (Port takes its name from the city of Oporto, which lies on the Douro River about 60 miles downstream from the mountain vineyards that produce the wine.)

Port is made in many styles. What makes it unique is that natural grape alcohol is added during fermentation—when the sugars of the grape are converted into alcohol. The result is a sweet but strong-tasting wine that is high in alcohol. Its quality is dependent upon the quality of a Douro vineyard's soil, the climate in a particular vintage, and the length of time it was allowed to age (which can be up to 40 years). Among the best-known styles are ruby Port, tawny Port, and vintage Port. Considered by many to be the best Port, vintage Port is often a blend of grapes from a single year from the best vineyards, and can be aged for more than 20 years.

Serve Port at room temperature. The classic accompaniments are walnuts and strong-flavored cheeses such as Stilton, Roquefort, or Gorgonzola. It is a fine afterdinner drink.

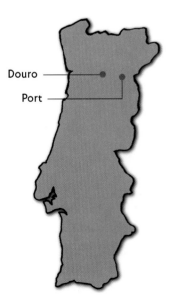

Douro

Port

Vinho Verde (literally "green wine") is a medium-dry, high-acidity wine best drunk chilled. The more expensive Vinho Verdes are made from the Alvarinho grape and have a more complex, longer-lasting flavor. Portugal's best red wine is Barca Velha from the Douro region, where Port is made. It is made with the Tinta Roriz varietal (Portugal's version of Tempranillo grapes). The result is a full-bodied, intense wine that requires years of aging.

german wines

*The rebirth of
Riesling and other
great wines*

German wines go in and out of fashion. Before World War II, they were considered to be among the best in the world and the signature tall, elegant German wine bottle was universally known. After the war, it sank out of favor—perhaps due to anti-German sentiment combined with mass exportation of very sweet, not-well-made German wines. But times change, and the new generation of German wines are absolutely delightful.

Almost all German wines are white, and the best are made with the celebrated and noble Riesling grape—a temperamental grape (see page 33) that ripens best in south-facing vineyards . It represents only about a quarter of all German wine plantings. More prolific than Riesling is Müller-Thurgau, which yields a softer, more rounded and fragrant wine. Other important grapes are Silvaner, Kerner, Scheurebe, and Rülander (the German name for Pinot Gris/Pinot Grigio).

As a result of Germany's reunification, the country now boasts 13 wine regions, 11 of which are in the west and two in the east. Most celebrated are the Rheingau, Rheinhessen, and Rheinpfalz regions on the banks of the Rhine River, and the Mosel-Saar-Ruwer region. These regions are all in western Germany and together produce a large portion of Germany's Riesling grapes. Wines from Mosel are easily recognizable because they come in green bottles, rather than the brown bottles used for almost all other German wines.

Like France, Germany has strict and complicated wine regulations. Unlike French rules that grade vineyards by region, German laws rank wine according to levels of ripeness of the grape at harvest time—with the ripest grapes being assigned the highest rank. These six levels are usually listed on a German wine label: Kabinett, Spätlese, Auslese, Beerenauslese, Eiswein, and Trockenbeerenauslese. The last three are the latest of the late-harvest grapes and produce very reduced quantities of sweet juice and intensely sweet wines.

ASK THE EXPERTS

Why is Germany famous for its dessert wines?

Germany's dessert wines are its most legendary wines. Beerenauslese (shortened to BA) and Trockenbeerenauslese (referred to as TBA) are considered Germany's greatest contributions to the world of wine. These wines are ranked the highest on the Prädikat level of quality. Both have been infected with "noble rot" (or the Botrytis cinerea fungus) in a special process. They are luscious and quite sweet, with fruit (apricot, peach, orange) and honey flavors. The best of these wines are made from Riesling grapes, although excellent examples are also made from Gewürztraminer, Scheurebe, and Silvaner grapes.

other old world wines

Unique wines that symbolize their regions

Austria

Austrian wine is made primarily from the white Grüner Veltliner variety, which accounts for about 30 percent of the vineyards. This variety produces many types of wines, from light, dry herbal wines to sweet, honeyed late-harvest wines. As in Germany, top-quality Austrian vineyards plant Riesling and make wines that are reminiscent of both the best German and the best Alsatian wines. Wines are also made from Weissburgunder (Pinot Blanc), Grauburgunder (Pinot Gris), and Sauvignon Blanc grapes. Austria also makes some of the finest late-harvest dessert wines in the world, many equal to those of Germany.

Greece

Let's not forget the Greeks, who didn't invent wine but have been producing and celebrating it for at least 3,000 years—and probably longer. Their traditional wine, called retsina, is an acquired taste because it is treated with the resin from pine trees that gives it a turpentine-like flavor and aroma. Although this may sound like an odd additive, resin was used by ancient Greeks and Romans as a preservative. Retsina simply continues a very old tradition. It comes in white and rosé varieties, and is best served chilled.

Switzerland

Switzerland makes white wine, much of which is produced from the Chasselas grape, which is also grown to a small degree in France. Switzerland also makes wines from Pinot Noir, Gamay, and Merlot grapes. Many experts consider Swiss wines to be quite delicious, although they tend to be expensive due to high production costs and the high value of Swiss currency to the dollar.

Hungary

Hungary has an old and prestigious winemaking history. The most important Hungarian wines are whites from the Transdanubia region made with locally grown grapes, such as Furmint. Hungary also produces dependable, full-bodied red wine. The most distinguished wines are made from the botrytis-infected Furmint from Tokay and known as the Tokay Eszencia. This rare and very expensive dessert wine is comparable to the best German Trockenbeerenausleses.

wines of argentina & chile

Where red Malbec grapes reign

Argentina is South America's biggest grape producing country, with annual production levels similar to the U.S.'s. The most famous red grape of Argentina is Malbec, a grape that was originally grown in France, where it was considered a blending grape. In Argentina it stands as its own wine, but is also used to blend with other grape varieties. Argentines also grow the Mission grape (popular in California in the 19th century), which they call the Criolla. Italian immigrants to Argentina brought with them Barbera, Lambrusco (not to be confused with North America's native vitis labrusca), Sangiovese, and Nebbiolo grapes. French rootstock—Pinot Noir, Syrah, Cabernet Sauvignon, and Merlot—also do well in the high country's arid climate. Argentina is renowned for red wine but also produces varietal whites: Chenin Blanc, Chardonnay, and sparkling wines are the favorites.

Chile is also a superb wine grape country. Yet until the 1980s, Chilean wine was relatively unknown to the outside world due to slow marketing practices and the unstable political situation. However, French varietals were long ago introduced to Chile. Like Argentina, Chile is red wine country. Cabernet Sauvignon and Merlot are the red celebrities. White grape varieties include Sauvignon Blanc, Sémillon, and Riesling.

CHILE

ARGENTINA

Mendoza

Argentina is a land of climatic and geographical extremes spanning rainforests and frigid mountains. In between the extremes lies the arid, heavily irrigated Mendoza province—in the shelter of the towering Andes. It is the center of Argentine grape growing.

ASK THE EXPERTS

Is Argentine wine as good as its beef?

Try a robust Argentine Malbec wine with some of that country's excellent beef. You'll find it a superb accompaniment—and further proof of how great cuisine goes well with great wine.

Aren't Argentine and Chilean wines pretty similar?

Although they grow some similar grape varieties, Argentina grows more Italian varietals, while Chile grows more French grapes. There's also a big difference in the structure of each country's wine business. The Penaflor winery dominates Argentine production, whereas Chile's wineries, known as bodegas, are mostly small family operations. Concha y Toro is Chile's largest winery, exporting an inexpensive Cabernet Sauvignon and Sauvignon Blanc that does well in the U.S.

PETER SELECTS

ARGENTINA
- **Catena Chardonnay**
Mendoza $16-$19

- **Catena Cabernet Sauvignon**
Mendoza $10-$19

- **Trapiche Malbec**
Mendoza $9-$11

CHILE–RED
- **Los Vascos Cabernet Sauvignon**
Colchagua Valley $8-$11

- **Los Vascos 1997**
Cabernet Sauvignon Reserve
Colchagua Valley $13-$15

- **Casa Lapostolle Cabernet Sauvignon Cuvée Alexandre**
Rapel Valley $18-$20

- **Casa Lapostolle Merlot Cuvée Alexandre**
Rapel Valley $22-$25

CHILEAN VALUE WINES–RED
- **Concha y Toro Cabernet Sauvignon**
$5-$7

- **Clos Robert Merlot**
$5-$8

- **Montes Special Cuvée Merlot**
$8-$10

- **Dallas Conte Cabernet**
$9-$11

CHILEAN VALUE WINES–WHITE
- **Concha y Toro Chardonnay "Blend"**
$5-$6

- **Concha y Toro Sauvignon Blanc**
$4-$5

- **Viña Anita Sémillon**
"Old Vine" Reserve $6-$8

- **Los Vascos Sauvignon Blanc**
$6-$9

wines of australia
& new zealand

*Red and white
down under*

Australia and New Zealand may be geographically remote from Europe's wine regions, but since 1990 both countries have been making tremendous inroads into English and North American wine markets. Australia grows no native grapes and has depended on imported European rootstock since the 19th century, particularly the Syrah (they call it Shiraz) grape from France's Rhône Valley.

Australia has a number of growing regions and microclimates that are similar to several of California's regions. A large portion of the country's wine grapes are grown near the capital, Adelaide, where the warm, dry climate fosters the famous red Shiraz and Cabernet Sauvignon grapes and inhibits pests. Cooler, higher parts of the region produce Chardonnay, Riesling, and Sauvignon Blanc. Two wine-producing states in the southeast, Victoria and New South Wales, and the state of Western Australia produce all the major vinifera grapes—grapes made famous by French winemakers.

Australia's smaller southern neighbor, New Zealand, is a relative new-comer on the wine scene but is catching up fast. Like Australia, its rootstock is entirely European—and Europeans run many of the country's wineries as well. The warmer North Island is known for its red grapes, particularly Cabernet Sauvignon, grown in the regions of Hawkes Bay and around Auckland. The cooler South Island is noted for Chardonnay and Sauvignon Blanc grapes.

SK THE EXPERTS

What is Shiraz? Is this an indigenous Australian variety?
Shiraz is actually the name for Syrah down under. So no, it is not native to Australia. Syrah comes from the northern Rhône Valley of France.

Why has Shiraz become so popular?
Shiraz is a big, fruity, flavorful red that can taste of blackberries, plums, and black cherries, and sometimes has leathery and earthy undertones. Australia has taken the French Syrah grape of France's northern Rhône Valley and made it uniquely its own. Most inexpensive Shirazes are mellow, fruity, and ready to drink upon release. They are best served with roasted meats.

Rosemount Estate Shiraz

PETER SELECTS

AUSTRALIA—RED
- **Deakin Estate Shiraz,**
  McLaren Vale, Australia
  $9-$10
- **Stonehaven Shiraz-Cabernet,**
  Southeast Australia,
  $9-$10
- **Rosemount Estate Shiraz Diamond Label Series**
  $10-$15
- **Coriole Shiraz**
  McLaren Vale, $20-$22

- **Peter Lehmann Eight Songs Shiraz**
  Barossa Valley $50

AUSTRALIA—WHITE
- **Lindemans Bin 65 Chardonnay,**
  Southeast Australia $8-$10
- **Black Opal Chardonnay,**
  Southeast Australia $9-11
- **Rosemount Chardonnay Diamond Label**
  Southeast Australia
  $10-$12

NEW ZEALAND—RED
- **Te Mata Estate Cabernet/Merlot**
  Hawkes Bay, New Zealand
  $20

NEW ZEALAND—WHITE
- **Babich Sauvignon Blanc,**
  Marlborough, New Zealand
  $10-$12
- **Brancott Chardonnay Reserve Gisborne,**
  New Zealand $14-$16

wines of south africa

No longer isolated

South Africa's climate and terrain are ideal for grape growing—a happy discovery made by European settlers, who by the 18th century were producing wine for export to Europe. The workhorse grape of South Africa was (and remained until recently) Steen, the local name for Chenin Blanc. This grape produced sweet and semi-sweet white and sparkling wines that were locally popular. The dominant red grape was Cinsaut, a cross between a Pinot Noir and another, lesser-known, grape, and is used to create Pinotage, a light red reminiscent of a hearty Beaujolais.

With the abolition of apartheid and the election of Nelson Mandela, South Africa has lost much of its insular status. Wine exports are increasing with significant sales of Port, Sherry, and fortified wines.

PETER SELECTS

RED

● **Fleur Du Cap Merlot,**
Coastal Region $8-$10

● **Fleur Du Cap Pinotage,**
Coastal Region $10-$12

● **Swartland Merlot,**
Coastal Region $10-$12

WHITE

● **Fleur Du Cap Chardonnay,**
Stellenbosch $8-$10

● **Thelema Sauvignon Blanc,**
Stellenbosch $18-$20

● **Mulderbosch Chardonnay,**
Stellenbosch, $23-$25

● **Mulderbosch
Sauvignon Blanc,**
Stellenbosch $20-$22

Increasingly, farmers are planting Merlot and Cabernet Sauvignon, but the venerable Steen remains the white grape responsible for the country's good, inexpensive white table wine.

Almost all of South Africa's grapes come from ten wine districts near the southwestern coast in idyllically beautiful Cape Province, near Cape Town. The climate is warm and dry. Damaging frosts and slashing rains are rare, and irrigation is widespread. All the natural ingredients favor a bright future for South African wine.

SK THE EXPERTS

Does South Africa host any wine events?

For sipping wine, you'll want to make the trip in March when Cape Town hosts the Nederburg wine auction, as it has done for the last 25 years. The auction is held at Nederburg Winery, the region's best-known cellar. Europeans and North Americans arrive to bid on Cabernet Sauvignon, Riesling, Gewürztraminer, and Edelkeur—a renowned dessert wine made from a Steen/Riesling blend.

answers to common questions

How can you locate wines from some of the more obscure wine-producing regions?

Ask your local wine shop to assist you. They may be able to special-order wine for you. Also, check the Internet. Several online wine stores stock wide selections.

How much wine can you bring back from a European trip?

The amount you spent for the wine you purchased counts against your customs dollar allowance—just as with any other items you bought. However, you will have to pay Federal duty and state sales tax on any quantity over one liter.

Why do Germany, Austria, and Switzerland mainly produce whites while Portugal, Spain, and Italy mainly produce reds?

Both whites and reds, of course, are grown in these countries, but the generalization holds. The reason is that different climates favor different types of grapes. The cooler European climate north of the Alps favors white wine grapes. The warmer and sunnier weather along the Mediterranean and Atlantic coasts favors reds.

What do you drink Cava with?

This Spanish sparkling wine is earthier than traditional sparkling wines. Flavorful, economical, and widely available, it is a good choice when entertaining large groups—especially if price is a consideration. Cava is also a perfect mixer for punches or mimosas (orange juice and sparkling wine.)

The recipe I am making calls for dry Sherry but I don't have any. I have some Madeira and Port—will they do?

The short answer is no. Each of these fortified wines has unique flavors that can't be substituted. It would be like substituting almond extract for vanilla extract. It might work in some cases, but certainly not in all.

How long will an open bottle of Port, Madeira or Sherry last?

Most open bottles of fortified wine will keep for up to one year. Madeira keeps the longest, dry Sherry the shortest.

HELFPUL RESOURCES

BOOKS

Windows on the World:
Complete Wine Course
By Kevin Zraly
Sterling Publications
Maps, facts and anecdotes about
wines around the world abound in
this attractive and accessible book

Parker's Wine Buyer's Guide, Fifth
Edition
By Robert M. Parker, Jr. .
Simon & Schuster
Complete easy-to-use reference on
recent vintages, prices, and ratings
for more than 8,000 wines from all
over the world.

Moët-Hachette International
Wine Dictionary
Hachette Publications
1500 words about wine in six
languages. Everything you need to
know about wine in English,
French, German, Italian, Spanish,
and Japanese.

WEB SITES

winepros.com
Australian wines are the focus with
articles by two of Australia's most
respected wine experts

10

Adding Wine to Your Life

if you like chardonnay, then try...

Getting started on expanding your wine palate

Developing a taste for wine gives new meaning to learning by doing. However, no other subject is as much fun to practice ! The operative word for doing is "tasting." That means tasting different wines and comparing and contrasting each with the other. Your exploration can begin by branching out from wines you like to similar ones that you may not have tried before. Here are some examples:

IF YOU LIKE . . .	THEN TRY
California Chardonnay	White Burgundy
California Cabernet Sauvignon	Red Bordeaux, Australian and South American Cabernet
Full-bodied reds	Malbec, Shiraz, Merlot, Barolo
Light, dry whites	Sauvignon Blanc, Sancerre
Champagne	California sparkling wine, Spanish Cava

You can try these different types of wine on your own by ordering wines by the glass at restaurants, at tastings, or on wine trips. As you do, you'll fine-tune your tasting skills by branching out from favorite **styles** (full-bodied or light) or **varietals** (wines named for their grape, such as Merlot or Cabernet Sauvignon).

FIRST PERSON DISASTER

Expensive lesson

I confess, I never really liked wine. The few times I tried it, it tasted sort of bitter. My girlfriend kept saying that maybe I needed to try some really good wine to change my mind. So on our anniversary I went to the wine store and bought the most expensive bottle of wine they had. A Château something-or-other from 1970. The wine store owner was impressed, as was my girlfriend. Then I poured a glass and tasted it. Wow! It sure was different from what I thought wine tasted like. She said it was the best thing she had ever tasted and added that if I didn't want to go broke, I'd better educate my taste buds on some less expensive wines.

—Mark T., Wilmington, Delaware

vintage wines

Rating wines by their vintages

The vintage of a wine refers to the year in which the grapes used to make it were grown. As with any other crop, the quality and quantity of grapes can vary year to year due to the vagaries of weather. These changes will in turn affect the quality of the wine made from those grapes. During a bad year, for example, a vineyard may experience a drought or heavy rains that affect how the grapes ripen. Even if the conditions haven't changed from spring to fall, a cold snap just a few days before the grapes are harvested can radically change the flavor of the grapes. The wines made during that year may not be as good as the same wines produced during another year when the weather was more cooperative.

The best vintage years are the good years in a particular wine's history. That means the grapes were the best and the wine the finest. Who determines which years are vintage and which aren't? Good question. Expert winetasters, for the most part. Each year they rate wines according to a whole slew of criteria (taste, tannin, color, bouquet, balance). If the wines from a particular region grown in a particular year are deemed superior, that year is considered a top vintage for that region. Most wine stores should have a vintage chart for the major wine regions of Europe and California.

Knowing a good (or a bad) vintage date for your favorite wines—or for the very best wines—may help you when you want to buy (or avoid) other wines. In a "good" year, very often many wines, including lesser ones, have benefited from the excellent weather conditions. These wines are therefore worth buying, even if they need to be aged. Similarly, a very bad year can affect a whole region— signaling that you should avoid those vintages where possible.

A "rare" or "fine" vintage refers to an old and special wine, such as a vintage Barolo from the early 20th century or an 18th-century vintage Madeira. They are also likely to be very expensive wines.

PETER SELECTS

- **Bordeaux**
  Best vintages since
  1961: '82, '85, '86, '89, '90,
  '95, '96, '98
- **Burgundy**
  Best vintages for
  White burgundies: '96, '97
- **California**
  Best recent vintages:
  '91, '94, '95, '96, '97, '99
- **Italy**
  Best recent vintages:
  '96, '97
- **Australia**
  Best recent vintage: '98

winetasting & trips

Tasting at the source

Are you finding that the more you learn about wine, the more you want to know? Great. Stretch your knowlege by taking an adult education class in wine. These classes are usually taught by local wine experts at a local college or university. Or if you live in or near a winegrowing region, even a relatively small one, most of the local wineries will also offer classes. Restaurants even get into the act, especially if the owner or chef is an expert in wine and wants to showcase the restaurant's wines.

Less formal but equally instructive are winetastings at local wine shops and gourmet food stores that are often announced in your local paper. Such winetastings attract people of all levels of knowledge. Bear in mind, however, that they are often designed to sell something (usually the wine).

Possibly the most all-engrossing way to learn about wine is to take a trip to the region where the wine is produced—whether it's reachable by a morning car ride or a flight across the ocean. Touring a wine region is probably the most delightful way to connect with its wineries.

ASK THE EXPERTS

Where can you locate a wine program near your home?
For the name of a wine school or an individual who offers wine programs in your area, contact the Society of Wine Educators in Savage, MD. (301-776-8569)

Can you learn a local cuisine while tasting its wine?
A number of international food and wine classes are available. These classes teach basic cooking techniques of the region (be it Italy, France, or Germany) and offer tastings of local wines. These courses usually last two or three weeks, long enough for a relaxing holiday but short enough for an annual vacation. For a listing of such trips, check the classified ads in the back of a good wine magazine, such as *The Wine Specatator,* sold at most major wine stores.

hosting a wine-tasting at home

Not everybody needs to be an expert

A casual winetasting party can be great fun—and an easy and festive way to get together with friends and learn more about wine. A small party—usually six to ten people—works best, rather like an intimate dinner party. Ask each person to bring a wine based upon a theme. In other words, focus on one kind of wine (Cabernets, Rieslings, Sherry, Champagne, etc.). The more specific the theme, the better. In addition, put some limit on the price range (such as under $20 per bottle).

As host or hostess, you too should supply a bottle. Also have plenty of sparkling water and finger food available, such as cheese and crackers, to help enhance the winetasting experience. Put everybody's wine on the table, with lots of glasses or plastic cups. Then serve each bottle, one after the other. You can make it into a contest and see who can guess the price of each wine or its region. At some home tastings, the host supplies a list of the wines to be tasted, wraps each bottle in foil, and gives it a number. The goal is to match the number to its correct wine. At the end of the evening, you can reveal the names of the wines. If you've made it a contest, the winner with the most correct answers gets a bottle of wine to take home.

After the second or third glass, everyone should be able to describe the characteristics of what they are drinking. Even wine innocents will have opinions that may enhance your appreciation of a particular wine. You'll learn a great deal about the wines, and have a very enjoyable evening.

WINETASTING PARTY IDEAS
You could hold a tasting party once a month

A Varietals Party

Focus on a particular varietal: Cabernet Sauvignon, Chardonnay, Syrah, Riesling, etc. It might be fascinating to learn that perhaps a certain South African Chardonnay is every bit as good as the California wine you've been drinking. You might also want to narrow the focus a bit and be specific about the region. For example, you might ask everyone to bring a California Chardonnay or an American Chardonnay.

Regional Wines Party

Tasting different wines from different regions means thinking about how "terroir" (soil and climate) affects a wine's flavor. Throw a party featuring one of each of the following: Red Bordeaux, White Burgundy, Vouv-ray, Sancerre, Australian Shiraz, Northern Italian red, Alsatian Gewürtraminer, etc.

A Sparkling Party

You could taste just Champagnes (inexpensive, very expensive), or just California sparklers. Or, using French Champagne as the benchmark, taste other sparklers from around the world in comparison.

Late-Harvest Dessert Party

On a cold winter evening, tasting sweet wines after a light supper would make a delightful party. You might use a good Sauternes as the benchmark to compare late-harvest wines from other regions of France or from around the world.

wine-buying
strategies

*Now you need
a plan*

If you become seriously interested in wine, you may want to become a collector. Most small collectors keep about 50 to 75 bottles of different wine on hand—that's about 4 to 6 cases. A good collection is well-rounded with reds, whites, middle-range wines, top wines, sparklers, dessert wines, and one or two fortified wines. In addition to the pleasure of collecting interesting wines, there is the convenience of having even a modest wine collection—you'll always have wine on hand when you need it.

Crafting a blueprint for your collection can be simple or difficult. It can be as easy as choosing a few favorite brands and sticking with them or as complex as collecting **verticals** (the wine term for collecting every vintage of a particular wine), for example, Joseph Phelps Napa Valley Cabernet Sauvignons produced from 1987 to 1997.

In general, you need to consider the following:

Your Tastes. This is always the most important criterion. Do you prefer mostly white wines or mostly reds? Light-bodied or full-bodied? Do you favor French wines? California wines?

Your Needs. Do you drink a bottle of wine every night at dinner, or do you consume only one or two bottles per week? Do you usually cook dishes that go better with white wine or with red? Do you entertain frequently? What sorts of meals do you prepare for company? Do you like to give wine as a gift?

Your Storage Facilities. How much wine can you store safely? If you live in a small apartment, perhaps 12 bottles may be all you can comfortably keep on hand at any one time. If you live in a house with a full cellar, perhaps you can keep 200 or more. Wine needs to be stored lying on its side in racks. It needs to be kept in a dark, fairly cool room, for instance, a basement or closet. Ideally, the temperature in that room should not vary too greatly because, over time, it can spoil the wines.

THE ART OF COLLECTING
Be the creator of your own collection

If you prefer Sancerre to Chardonnay or Merlot to Cabernet:

Don't let the snobs push you into collecting wines you won't like. You will be drinking them.

If you find a label you really like:

Buy as much as you can. For everyday wine, you'll want to be sure you have it on hand. If it's a wine that will improve with aging, you'll want to have as much as you can afford and have the space to store.

If you've gotten your favorite wines "under control" and you're ready to experiment:

Begin to buy other wines that have the same styles and flavors that you like. For example, if you like California Cabernets, try Australian Shirazes. Begin to introduce new wines into your collection.

If you've been keeping wine on hand for a long time:

Most wines can be drunk when they're sold. Aging wine adds new dimensions to its flavors and textures, but don't wait too long. Most reds shouldn't exceed 15 years, and whites 3 years.

buying wine as an investment

Buying wine now to sell at a profit later

The theory behind investing in any art or antique is that its value will increase with time. The same goes for wine. Unfortunately, because wine is so perishable—certainly more perishable than a Chippendale chair—buying wine as an investment can be risky.

If you seriously want to buy wine for investment purposes, rule one is to seek advice from an expert. A seasoned professional in the wine business will know potential pitfalls and will steer you in the right direction. Also consult respected journals and books for recommended wines.

Invest only in wines with a reputation for long-term value. Obviously, you will be looking for wines that will age well, so only go for those from superlative vintages or for wines that have a long track record for becoming more valuable over time. Also look for wines that may eventually become rare, such as wines produced in small amounts from prestigious wineries.

Of course, you might want to buy an investment-quality wine to drink. For example, you may want to buy a very old Madeira to give to an uncle who is a Revolutionary War scholar. The best advice is to buy such wines only from a reputable dealer. Not only will this assure you that your wine was stored properly (ensuring that it is still good), it also offers security. If it turns out to be bad, you can return it.

You should have no problem bringing back a bad wine as long as you do so within a reasonable length of time. After all, good wine merchants are in business to please consumers. If too much time has passed, the dealer will wonder how you stored this very special wine.

ASK THE EXPERTS

What is a wine auction?

Just like antique or art auctions, a wine auction is a place where valuable wines are sold to the highest bidders. Laws concerning buying and selling wine by auction vary in each state, but auctions are legal in California, Illinois, and New York. Wine auctions are a good place to find very rare wines. Wine auctioneers typically add a buyer's premium of from 10 to 15 percent to each sale.

Other than an auction, how else can I invest in wine?

Buy wine futures. Here, you pay a discounted price in advance of a wine's delivery. The idea is that the price paid for futures is lower than the price of the wine when it is released. Then when the wine arrives, it can be sold for profit. Again, this is an extremely risky financial venture. Wine futures should be purchased only from the most reputable wine merchants.

answers to common questions

How do you store wine at home?

Whether you live in a two-room apartment or a 20-room house, today it is possible to have a wine cellar (or perhaps a wine closet) at home. All that's necessary is a dark, undisturbed place under constant cool (50 to 65 degrees F) temperatures. Store the bottles horizontally (stack cases on their sides) to ensure that the corks remain moist and airtight. Some wine stores and wine-accessory merchants offer self-contained wine closets. They vary in size from holding 60 bottles to 1000 or more. Carefully assess your future needs before ordering one of these units—most collectors find themselves running out of room as their penchant for wine collecting grows.

When I store an opened bottle in my refrigerator, should I lay it down?

Once a bottle has been opened, it's best to store the remaining wine standing up in the refrigerator so that the surface of the wine within the bottle comes into less contact with the air inside the bottle. Don't put the bottle in the door of the fridge, for every time you open and close the door, you'll be sloshing the wine around, helping it to deteriorate faster.

I've seen wine decanted. When should I decant and in what?

Decanters are merely glass vessels used to aerate young wines and leave the sediment behind in old ones. Some experts decant almost everything red; but if you wish to do so, remember that it's not necessary to spend a lot on the decanter. In lieu of decanting, most wine enthusiasts will open a red wine 30 minutes to one hour before serving it to let it breathe. This is not done with whites.

HELPFUL RESOURCES

The Wine Advocate
by Robert M. Parker, Jr.
This is perhaps the best-known and most prestigious newsletter by one of the world's most influential wine experts. Annual subscription: $45. For subscription information, call: 410-329-6477.

The Vine
by Clive Coates
An authority on wines of Burgundy and Bordeaux, Coates writes for the advanced wine connoisseur. For subscription information, e-mail: clive.coates@care4free.net.

Stephen Tanzer's International Wine Cellar
by Stephen Tanzer
Written and published six times a year with sophisticated, insightful, and expert consumer wine-buying advice keyed to market conditions and regional vintages. Extensive tasting notes and ratings. Annual subscription: $54. For subscription information, write to: Tanzer Business Communications P.O. Box 20021 Cherokee Station, NY 10021

WEB SITE

www.morrellandcompany.com
The Web site of Morrell and Company provides extensive information about wine, including upcoming wine auctions.

glossary

acid A compound present in all grapes and an essential component of wine that preserves it, enlivens and shapes its flavors, and helps prolong its aftertaste.

aeration The process of letting a wine "breathe" in the open air by swirling the wine in a glass, which can soften young, tannic wines.

aftertaste (See also finish.) The taste of flavors that linger in the mouth after the wine is tasted. The most important factor in judging a wine's character and quality. Great wines have rich, long, complex aftertastes.

alcohol A chemical compound formed by the action of yeast on the sugar content of grapes during fermentation. Most wines have between 7 and 25 percent alcohol, which gives wine is vinosity. If wine has too much alcohol for its body weight, it is unbalanced, and will taste uncharacteristically heavy or hot. The quality will be noticeable in aroma and aftertaste.

American Viticulture Area (AVA) A geographical grape-growing area that has officially been given appellation status in the United States by the U.S. Bureau of Alcohol, Tobacco, and Firearms. Examples: Napa Valley, Finger Lakes.

American oak (See also French Oak.) The alternative to French oak for making wine barrels. Used by many California, Spanish, and Australian winemakers primarily for aging Cabernet Sauvignon, Merlot, and Zinfandel. Provides strong vanilla and cedar flavors. Not as popular or prestigious as French Oak, but is about half the price.

appearance Refers to a wine's clarity, not its color.

appellation A French word that defines the area where a wine's grapes were grown (Bordeaux, Mosel, Sonoma), and can be as small as a chateau (Château Lafitte Rothschild). Regulations vary widely from country to country, state to state, and region to region with regard to whether and in what manner the appellation can be used on a label. For example, in California, to print the state on the label (California Chardonnay), 100 percent of the grapes must have been grown in California. However, for the region's name (Napa Valley) to appear on the label, only 85 percent of the grapes must have been grown in the specified district.

Appellation d'Origine Contrôlée (AOC or AC) The French system of appellations, begun in the 1930s and considered the wine world's benchmark.

aroma (Also: bouquet.) The smell that the grapes, fermentation, and oak aging impart to a wine.

austere Relatively hard, high-acid wines that lack depth and roundness. Usually said of young whites.

backbone Describes wines that are full-bodied, well structured, and balanced, especially due to a correct level of acidity.

balance Describes wines that are harmonious with no single dominating element; it refers to the ratio among the different characteristics of a wine, including fruitiness, acidity, tannin, content, alcoholic strength.

barrel fermented Wine that has been fermented in small casks instead of large tanks. Experts believe that barrel fermentation contributes greater harmony in the wine, increases body, and adds complexity, texture, and flavor.

blanc de blancs French for "white of whites," and

refers to a French Champagne that is made totally of Chardonnay grapes instead of the traditional blending of Pinot Noir (a red variety) with Chardonnay.

blanc de noirs French for "white of blacks," and describes a rare white Champagne made from red (black) grapes where the juice is not put in contact with the black skins.

blend Nearly every wine is made by blending in other grape varieties (even to a tiny degree) or other vintages; fortified wines are by definition blended.

body Used to describe the impression of weight or fullness on the palate; usually expressed as full-bodied, medium-bodied, or light-bodied.

botrytis cinerea A beneficial mold or fungus that attacks grapes under certain climatic conditions and causes them to shrivel, concentrating their flavors, sugar, and acids. Sauternes (Château d'Yquem) is probably the most famous example. (See also late-harvest.)

botrysized Affected by the botrytis cinerea fungus.

bouquet See aroma. Traditionally the smell that a wine acquires from the grapes and from fermentation, but also the wine's total smell including those resulting from oak aging.

breathing What a wine does when it is exposed to air through decanting (see also decanting) or swirling. Opinions vary regarding whether or not breathing is beneficial to a wine.

brut Used to designate the driest Champagne or sparkling wine.

cava Spanish word for sparkling wine.

cave French word for cellar; used for small household wine coolers.

cellared by A phrase that means the wine was not produced at the winery where it was bottled.

chewy A descriptive term applied to rich, heavy, tannic wines that are full-bodied.

claret English term for a red Bordeaux.

corkage fee A charge a restaurant may apply when customers bring their own wines.

corky A description of a wine that has been contaminated by a rotting cork and implying an unpleasant smell and taste.

cuvée A blend or special lot of wine.

decanting The process of removing the sediment from a wine before drinking by carefully pouring wine from its bottle into another carafe or container.

dry Not sweet, no taste of sugar.

eiswein A sweet German wine made by harvesting frozen grapes during a frost and pressing them while they are still frozen.

estate bottled A term used by producers for those wines made from vineyards that they owned and that were part of the winery estate. Indicates that a winery either owns the vineyard or has a long-term lease from a particular vineyard.

fermentation The process that turns grape juice into wine. In fermentation, yeast converts sugar into alcohol and carbon dioxide.

finish (See also aftertaste.) The tastes that linger in the mouth after the wine is tasted, and the key to a wine's character. Great wines have long, complex finishes.

fortified Wines whose alcohol content has been increased by the addition of brandy or grape spirits.

French oak (See also American oak.) The traditional wood for wine barrels. French oak supplies vanilla, cedar, and other distinctive flavors to both red and white wines.

fresh Has a clean, lively character. An excellent quality for young, especially white, wines.

fumé Literally "smoky." The term refers to a tangy aroma of certain wines made from Sauvignon Blanc grapes, particularly Pouilly Fumé or Mondavi's Fumé Blanc.

grand cru Literally "great growth." The term means different things in different regions; in Burgundy it is the highest rank; in Bordeaux it is more universal; in some other regions of the world, it is used only on cheaper wines.

green Describes the taste of unripe fruit or early harvest grapes. It is a positive aspect of good German wines.

harsh A wine that has an astringent quality; too high in tannin or alcohol.

hearty A wine that is full-bodied, warm, and earthy. Often used to describe red wines that are high in alcohol.

heady A wine that is very high in alcohol.

hot A wine that is very high in alcohol to the point where it is unbalanced, although it is acceptable in Port wines.

jug wine Inexpensive, everyday wine that comes in large jugs.

late-harvest (See also botrytis cinerea.) Indicates that grapes were picked later in the season, when they contain more sugar than grapes harvested earlier. Associated with dessert wines.

maceration Steeping the grape skins and other solids during fermentation with the purpose of extracting color, tannin, and aroma from them.

malolactic fermentation A secondary fermentation that occurs in most wines and converts malic acid into softer lactic acid and carbon dioxide, reducing the wine's acidity. It softens red wines (Cabernet, Merlot), and adds complexity to hearty whites (Chardonnay).

mature When a wine is ready to drink.

méthode champenoise The labor-intensive and costly process whereby wine undergoes a secondary fermentation inside the bottle that creates bubbles or effervescence. All Champagne and most high-quality sparkling wines are made with this process.

négociant A French wine merchant who buys grapes from various winegrowers and makes wine, or buys various wines and blends them, then sells the product under his own name. Louis Jadot is a well-known négociant.

nonvintage or NV A wine blended from more than one vintage, allowing the vintner to establish a stable house style. Many Champagnes, sparkling wines, sherries, and ports are nonvintage.

nose (See also aroma and bouquet.) Another term to describe the way a wine smells.

nouveau A young, light, fruit-intensive wine; usually applied to Beaujolais.

nutty. Used negatively to describe oxidized wine (see also oxidized); used positively to describe an oaky flavor.

oaky Used to describe the taste imparted to a wine as a result of being aged in oak barrels.

oenology The study of wine.

off-dry Indicates a lightly sweet wine.

oxidized Describes wine that has been exposed

too long to air and has taken on a brownish color, losing freshness, and can develop a taste of old apples, old Madeira, or worse.

peak The moment when a wine is at its best.

premier cru In Bordeaux, wine from the best chateaux; in Burgundy, the term refers to the second grade of classed vineyard, the first being Grand Cru.

premium An American term for better wines.

private reserve (See also reserve.) Can indicate wines of excellent quality, but is not a regulated term, so essentially it means nothing.

rosé Pink wine made from black grapes pressed quickly so that only a light tinge of color affects the juice. Called rosato in Italy.

soft Used to describe wines that are low in acid, tannin, or both; opposite of hard.

spumante Italian word for sparkling.

table wine The general word for everyday wine. In Europe, European Economic Community (EEC) regulations rank it below Vin de Qualité Produits dans des Régions Déterminées or VQPRD. In the U.S., it is a generic term.

tannin The mouth-puckering substance, found mostly in red wine, that is derived from the grape's skin, seeds, and stems.

tasting note The brief description by a wine-tasting expert on how a wine appears, smells, and tastes.

terroir A French word meaning soil and site; a wine is said to have un goût de terroir (a taste of the soil) when it has gathered flavor from the land on which it was produced.

viniculture The science of grape production for wine and the making of wine.

vintage The year the wine was made. Laws vary in other countries, but in the United States, for a wine to carry a vintage date, 95 percent of it must come from grapes grown in that year.

vintner A wine merchant or wine producer.

viticultural area The legal or regulatory definition of a grape-growing region, which takes into account climate, soil, geographical features, definable boundaries, and other features. The defined viticultural area (Bordeaux, Napa Valley, etc.) affects the appellation of a wine. For example, in the U.S. 85 percent of grapes must come from the viticultural area (Napa Valley) for it to carry the appellation.

viticulture The cultivation, science, and study of grapes.

vitis labrusca Native North American species of grapes, including the Concord variety, used to make wine.

vitis vinifera Classic European species of grapes used to make wine, including the Cabernet Sauvignon and Chardonnay varieties, among others.

yeast Micro-organisms that produce enzymes that convert sugar to alcohol; necessary for fermentation of grape juice into wine.

index

PICTURE CREDITS

Catherine Lazure illustrations 7, 25, 41, 57, 75, 89, 111, 129, 147, 167

Photos of wine bottles and glassware by **Robert Milazzo**, all other photos by **Photodisc**, except for the following: **Steve Budzynski** photo, courtesy **Sam's Wines and Spirits** 76; **Clicquot, Inc.** 114; **Banfi Vintners** 117 (bottom); **Courtesy Vinitaly, Veronafieri** 120; **Glenn Curtiss Museum, Hammondsport, NY** 130, 138; **Sebastiani** 134; **Bargetto Winery** 136; **Heron Hill Winery** 142; **ICEX, Foreign Trade Institute of Spain** 150; **ICEP, Portuguese Trade Commission** 152; **Brancott Vineyards** 160; **Bargetto Winery** 172

Barbara J. Morgan Editor

Barb Chintz Editorial director, the *Now What?!* series

Pamela Thomas Contributing writer

Robin Malik, Buddy Boy Design Interior design

Leonard Vigliarolo Cover design

Amla Sanghvi, Ann Stewart Picture research

Marguerite Daniels Editorial assistant

THE AUTHOR: UP CLOSE

I've been involved with wine most of my life. In fact, some people might even say that wine is my life. My father went into the wine business more than 80 years ago. In those days, most Americans were not particularly interested in wine. It was enjoyed mostly by either the very rich, or by working class immigrants who remembered the pleasure of wine from the old country. Then came Prohibition and the Depression, but my father's business managed to survive both. After World War II, he opened a retail wine shop in Manhattan, and as Americans began to appreciate wine more, the Morrell wine business took off.

After all these years, Morrell and Company remains a family business. I'm the Chairman, my sister Roberta is President, and Roberta's husband, Nikos Antonakeas, is Managing Director. My niece Ruth is in charge of our direct mail and catalog division, and my nephews Tony and Jon work here too.

We've had a wine shop in Manhattan since 1947, and recently opened a beautiful shop at One Rockefeller Plaza—in the heart of New York City. Our shop includes a wine bar—a great place to stop for both a light meal and to enjoy a delicious glass of wine—perhaps to taste something new. We offer over 100 choices of wine by the glass, from inexpensive Côtes du Rhônes, to elegant Bordeaux, to very special American Cabernets.

Come by and visit.

Or contact me at *www.morrellandcompany.com.* Anything I can do to enhance your enjoyment of wine would give me enormous pleasure.

Peter Morrell
Chairman
Morrell and Company